PICTURES OF
THE APOSTOLIC CHURCH

BY THE SAME AUTHOR

ST. PAUL THE TRAVELLER AND THE ROMAN CITIZEN. 10s. 6d.
THE CHURCH IN THE ROMAN EMPIRE BEFORE A.D 170. 12s.
A HISTORICAL COMMENTARY ON ST. PAUL'S EPISTLE TO THE GALATIANS. 12s.
THE LETTERS TO THE SEVEN CHURCHES OF ASIA. 12s.
PAULINE AND OTHER STUDIES. 12s
THE CITIES OF ST. PAUL. 12s.
LUKE THE PHYSICIAN. 12s.
WAS CHRIST BORN AT BETHLEHEM ? 5s.
THE EDUCATION OF CHRIST. 2s 6d.
THE REVOLUTION IN CONSTANTINOPLE AND TURKEY IN 1909. net 10s 6d.
IMPRESSIONS OF TURKEY. 6s.
STUDIES IN THE HISTORY AND ART OF THE EASTERN ROMAN PROVINCES. net. 20s.
and
THE THOUSAND AND ONE CHURCHES. By PROF. SIR W M RAMSAY and GERTRUDE L. BELL. net. 20s.

BY LADY RAMSAY

EVERYDAY LIFE IN TURKEY. 5s.
THE ROMANCE OF ELISAVET. 5s.

LONDON : HODDER AND STOUGHTON

PICTURES

OF THE

APOSTOLIC CHURCH

ITS LIFE AND TEACHING

BY

SIR WILLIAM M. RAMSAY

D.C.L., LL.D., D.D.

PROFESSOR OF HUMANITY IN THE UNIVERSITY OF ABERDEEN

WIPF & STOCK · Eugene, Oregon

Wipf and Stock Publishers
199 W 8th Ave, Suite 3
Eugene, OR 97401

Pictures of the Apostolic Church
Its Life and Teaching
By Ramsay, William M.
Softcover ISBN-13: 978-1-6667-3397-6
Hardcover ISBN-13: 978-1-6667-2933-7
eBook ISBN-13: 978-1-6667-2934-4
Publication date 8/12/2021
Previously published by Hodder and Stoughton, 1910

This edition is a scanned facsimile of
the original edition published in 1910.

PREFACE

THIS book consists of fifty-two Sections, fifty of which were written for "The Sunday School Times" in comment upon the International Lessons of 1909. Each is complete in itself; but the subjects were chosen so as to work together into a series of typical pictures of the life, the teaching, and the development of the early Church.

The length of treatment of these subjects was formerly determined by the exigencies of space in a periodical. In the present book the whole series is treated on a uniform scale, according to comparative importance in the history of the Church. The growth of the Church was determined by progressive revelation to the earliest Christians through the indwelling Spirit, and by clearer comprehension on their part of the Divine purpose. Perception of this principle guided Luke in selecting and grouping the facts which he records. He knew much that he did not incorporate in his history. He gave space in his pages to events and persons according as they influenced the growth of the Church; and the present writer tries simply to follow the scale set by Luke. Hence the almost complete omission of John the Apostle, whose activity, powerful as it was, lies in the end of the first century and therefore falls outside the limits of Luke's history.

The difference in relative scale between the original form of these studies and the present publication may be seen especially in the case of Stephen, to whom two Sections are now assigned. There was lacking also a connected sketch of the activity of Paul, and this has been added as the concluding Section.

It is necessary for the reader to remember that "Asia" in Luke denotes, not the vast continent of Asia, but the Roman province, a part of Asia Minor, lying between Galatia and the Ægean Sea. So it is used in the following pages. So also "Galatia" and "Macedonia" in these pages always denote the Roman provinces, not the countries or kingdoms which bore those names. Luke avoids the term "Galatia" on account of the ambiguity; but the Roman Paul uses the Roman term, and the Church from his time onwards made a practice of accepting the political facts and divisions of the Empire.

W. M. RAMSAY.

University of Aberdeen,
   17 *August,* 1910.

CONTENTS

	PAGE
PREFACE	v
INTRODUCTION: LUKE AND HIS MESSAGE	xi

SECTION

I. THE ASCENSION. *Acts* I. 1-14	1
II. THE DAY OF VISION AND POWER. *Acts* II. 1-21	5
III. THE BIRTH OF THE CHURCH. *Acts* II. 22-47	12
IV. THE POWER OF FAITH. *Acts* III. 1-26	17
V. THE SOURCE OF POWER. *Acts* IV. 1-31	23
VI. THOU SHALT NOT WRONG GOD. *Acts* IV. 32-V. 11	29
VII. THE TEST OF TRUTH. *Acts* V. 12-42	36
VIII. GOOD ORDER MAKES FOR ACTIVITY IN THE CHURCH. *Acts* VI. 1-7	42
IX. THE DEATH OF STEPHEN THE VICTORY OF THE CHURCH. *Acts* VI 8-VII. 60	47
X. TRUE AND FALSE BELIEF. *Acts* VIII. 1-24	54
XI. THE PROPHET IN THE WILDERNESS. *Acts* VIII. 25-40	63
XII. THE WORK AND POWER OF PETER. *Acts* IX. 32-43	70

CONTENTS

SECTION		PAGE
XIII.	The Cause and Manner of the Growth of the Church. *Review · Acts* i.-ix.	77
XIV.	The Universal Gospel. *Acts* x. 1-xi. 18	84
XV.	A Messenger of the Lord. *Acts* xii. 1-24	91
XVI.	The Conversion of Paul. *Acts* viii. 1; ix. 1-22	98
XVII.	Origin of the Greek Church. *Acts* xi. 19-30; xii. 25	105
XVIII.	The Approach to the Gentiles. *Acts* xiii. 1-12	112
XIX.	Paul turns to the Gentiles. *Acts* xiii. 13-52	120
XX.	The Churches of Galatia. *Acts* xiv. 1-30	127
XXI.	The Union of Jews and Gentiles in the Church. *Acts* xv. 1-35; *Gal* ii. 11 ff.	134
XXII.	Faith and Works. *James* ii. 14-26	141
XXIII.	Word and Act. *James* iii. 1-12	147
XXIV.	The Nature and Power of Faith. *Heb.* xi. 1-30	153
XXV.	Christianity giving Vitality to the Ancient Civilization. *Review: Acts* x.-xv.	159
XXVI.	The Motive Power of Life. *Rom.* xiii. 1-14	166
XXVII.	The Entrance of the Gospel into Europe. *Acts* xv. 36-xvi. 15	172
XXVIII.	The First Christian Church in Europe. *Acts* xvi 16-40	180
XXIX.	The Progress through Macedonia. *Acts* xvii. 1-15	187

CONTENTS

SECTION		PAGE
XXX.	PAUL AT ATHENS. *Acts* XVII. 16-34	194
XXXI.	THE CHARTER OF CHRISTIAN FREEDOM IN THE ROMAN EMPIRE. *Acts* XVIII. 1-18	201
XXXII.	ADVICE TO A NEWLY FORMED CHURCH. 1 *Thess.* v. 12-24	209
XXXIII.	THE IMPERIAL AIMS OF PAUL. *Acts* XVIII. 23-XIX. 22	215
XXXIV.	PAUL'S VICTORY OVER THE MOB IN EPHESUS. *Acts* XIX. 23-XX. 1	222
XXXV.	A HYMN OF LOVE THE DIVINE. 1 *Cor.* XIII. 1-13	229
XXXVI.	PAUL'S FAREWELL TO THE HELLENIC CHURCHES. *Acts* XX. 2-38	235
XXXVII.	THE PROPHETS WHO STOPPED PAUL. *Acts* XXI. 1-17	242
XXXVIII.	THE CHURCH AND ITS ENEMIES IN THE PAGAN WORLD. *Review Acts* XIV.-XXI.	249
XXXIX.	FREEDOM IN EVERYDAY LIFE. 1 *Cor.* X. 23-33	256
XL.	SELF-DENIAL THE PROOF OF LOVE. *Rom.* XIV. 10-21	263
XLI.	THE BEGINNING OF THE CRISIS. *Acts* XXI. 17-XXII. 29	271
XLII.	THE REAL ISSUE BETWEEN PAUL AND THE JEWS. *Acts* XXII. 30-XXIII. 35	279
XLIII.	PROGRESS OF PAUL'S CASE IN PALESTINE. *Acts* XXIV.	286
XLIV.	PAUL'S APPEAL TO CÆSAR. *Acts* XXV. and XXVI.	293
XLV.	PAUL TAKES COMMAND WHEN DANGER THREATENS. *Acts* XXVII. 1-26	301

CONTENTS

SECTION		PAGE
XLVI.	PAUL THE SAVIOUR OF HIS COMPANIONS. *Acts* XXVII. 27-XXVIII. 10	307
XLVII.	A LAST APPEAL TO THE JEWS. *Acts* XXVIII. 11-31	314
XLVIII.	WEAKNESS MADE STRONG: THE AUTOBIOGRAPHY OF A MISSIONARY. 2 *Cor.* XI. 18-XII. 10	320
XLIX.	THE LAW OF SPIRITUAL COMPENSATION. 2 *Cor.* VIII.	326
L.	PAUL'S LAST WILL AND TESTAMENT. 2 *Tim.* IV. 1-18	332
LI.	THE EPITAPH OF PAUL. 2 *Tim.* IV. 7	338
LII.	REVIEW OF THE INFLUENCE OF LOCAL CIRCUMSTANCES ON THE LIFE OF PAUL	344

INTRODUCTION

LUKE AND HIS MESSAGE

ANY reasonable discussion of the book of the Acts of the Apostles must rest on a definite opinion as to the evidence on which the narrative depends. Luke (as he tells us in his Gospel, chap. i. 1 f.) had many authorities. He follows the practice observed by writers of his age, and states simply the conclusions to which his consideration of his authorities had led him, without formally naming the source of his knowledge. But careful reading of his very careful narrative suggests in many cases what his authority was. The following pages are written on the view that in the opening chapters of the Acts Luke's chief authority was the belief and the accounts current in Christian circles, as he heard them in Jerusalem and Cæsarea when he was there with Paul for more than two years, A.D. 57-59. Taking A.D. 29 as the date of the Crucifixion, we find that this part of the narrative rests on evidence which was current within thirty years of the actual events, amid a society consisting largely of eye-witnesses and the children of eye-witnesses.

We can safely assume that Luke had been in communication with many Christians in both cities, that he had compared their accounts in a natural and unconscious way, and that these chapters present the sum of what he believed on this evidence. We cannot assume that, when he was in Palestine, he was intending to write a history and was consciously or critically comparing accounts; and above all we must not assume that his standard of judging was the same as ours. Though above the ordinary level of education and ability, he judged as a man of that age, a converted pagan, would judge. He states quite plainly that he wrote his history because he had enjoyed access to the best sources of information, and not that he had sought out information because he wished to write a history.

This may be regarded as an additional proof of the unbiassed character of his outlook, and of the unconscious and therefore perfectly honest way in which the narrative gradually took form in his mind. But at the same time it suggests that the general and spiritual truth would impress itself on his mind more deeply than the details.

The early history of the Christian Church is narrated by Luke as "miraculous," i.e. as resulting from the direct interposition of the Divine power on certain occasions. I accept this character, and try to preserve it in its proper proportions; but it would be a mistake to exaggerate it, and to have recourse to marvel where no marvel is apparent. It is not necessary to infer that every mention of an "angel," i.e. a messenger of God, implies supernatural agency. Any being, or power, or person, that served as an instrument to bring the Divine Will to its consummation, might be, and commonly was, regarded in Semitic thought as a "messenger of God".

But an element, which many persons in modern times stigmatize as "miraculous" and therefore incredible, is mingled inextricably with Luke's narrative, even in those parts where he was himself an eye-witness, and with all the books of the New Testament. We cannot eliminate those details which seem to us marvellous, and regard the rest as true. The history stands as a whole, and must be judged accordingly; and reason, history and evidence seem to the present writer to prove that it is true.

The tendency to disbelieve any history that contains a marvellous or miraculous element is largely due to prepossession. Much that superficial thinkers among us regard as "miraculous" is simply unfamiliar. Much that would have been ridiculed as incredible and absurd thirty years ago has now become familiar and accepted in modern science. It is an irrational prejudice to suppose that a thing is untrue because it is strange and unfamiliar. For the word "miraculous" we might substitute "superhuman," and we should recognize (as Luke recognized) that the relation between man and God necessarily moves on a plane that is superhuman.

There is no reason to think that the Acts of the Apostles was written as a separate work under that name. It was understood by the author as the Second Book of his history; and the reader will best understand it if he studies it in this way. It was probably at some time in the second century that the Second Book was separated from the First; and, while the First was placed as one of the Gospels, the Second, standing alone, required a name; and the title, "Acts of the Apostles," was invented for it. Yet its opening words show clearly that the writer thought of it as the second part of a single history.

I

THE ASCENSION

Acts i. 1-14

THE Acts, the second book of Luke's history, opens with a brief summary of the subject contained in his first book, and then gives a fuller statement of its final episode, the Ascension. This episode must be regarded as the climax and the necessary conclusion of the Saviour's life, as Luke sets it before us and as it must be frankly accepted or rejected. The central idea of the Christian religion, the idea which cannot be doubted or minimized without sacrificing the essential truth of Christianity, is that God, who had always through His messengers and prophets communicated His word to man, at last, as the climax of His grace, sent His only Son into the world. The Divine Nature, which is omnipresent and eternal, free from the human limitations of space and time, materialized itself in human form upon the earth, voluntarily subjecting itself to those limitations and yet continuing to be Divine. "The Word was made flesh, and dwelt among us." In so far as it was human, this expression of the Divine Nature in the world must have a beginning, a history for a term of years, and an end, i.e., a birth, life, and death. Yet, on the other hand, as being Divine, it was pre-existent and deathless. The Word was in the beginning, and the Word was God. Birth and death have no bearing on the eternal Divine Nature. Thus the Divine Nature makes itself in appearance to us double, and this double nature is called by the terms Father and Son, which must of course be regarded as symbolical names, attempting to make the Divine mystery intelligible to the human mind with its necessarily limited powers of understanding.

It was therefore an essential part of the Divine purpose, that those who had known the Divine Word in its human expression as the man Jesus, should become aware that death had no real power over Him. This result was accomplished by various events after such fashion that a sufficient number of persons were firmly convinced of the truth, and constituted a body of witnesses whose evidence might convince the world and give effect to the Divine will.

After this conviction was produced, we come to the final stage, the apparent departure of the embodied Divine Nature, the man Jesus, from the world. The earthly period had fulfilled its purpose and reached its climax. This is the Ascension. This term, like many of the other words which must be employed by man in discussing the subject, is an attempt to express Divine truth—which as Divine is not subject to worldly conditions—in the language of human imperfection. The Divine Nature is omnipresent. It does not lie more in one direction from us than in another; it is neither above nor below: it is everywhere. To say that Jesus went up into heaven is a merely symbolic expression; it has not a local significance; it is an emblematic statement of the truth. The truth which has to be conceived in the mind is that, at the due stage and the proper moment, Jesus ceased to be apparent to human senses in the world, and *is* God with God.

In Acts I. 1-14 Luke assumes that his readers know the briefer account of the Ascension already given by him in his Gospel (XXIV. 44-51). He does not in Acts mention that the event occurred on the Mount of Olives. That was known, and is here presumed in verse 12. That there are slight apparent differences in details between the two accounts will trouble no one who thinks in the same fashion as Luke and the men of his age thought. Luke puts the accounts side by side; the spiritual truth was the one important thing; differences of detail were unreal. Similarly he describes Paul's conversion three times, always with slight differences in details. Truths transcendental and Divine had to be expressed in the insufficient language of mankind, and made intelligible to men of that time. It is part of Luke's intention to leave the accompaniments vague, shadowy and uncertain, in order to concentrate attention on what was real, spiritual and certain

But why were two accounts of the Ascension given in two books of the same historical work by one author? The Ascension is not merely the suitable end of the Gospel. It is also the beginning of the history of Christianity as set forth in the Acts. The work of men was now to begin, where the work of the Son of God on earth ended. The very first episode in this new stage of the history is the demonstration that this Ascension, this departure of the Divine incarnate Word, is only apparent, not permanent. Jesus leaves the world with the promise to return. The Divine Nature never leaves man alone to himself. It is always with him. That this is so, and how the disciples learned in actual experience that it is so, is the next episode in Acts, and the next step in the education of the disciples for the work which they had to perform in the world.

II

THE DAY OF VISION AND POWER

Acts II. 1-21

WE have realized why it was that the Son of God must bring His work in this world to an end, and must depart when His work on earth had been completed. This departure, however, is, in a sense, only apparent and not real. It was the end of the period during which the Divine Nature, as the Word become flesh, subjected itself to the human limitations of space and time. But the Divine Nature in itself is never absent from the world or removed from it; it is always everywhere. Jesus himself in His life on earth had assured the disciples that He was with them always, even unto the end of the world. He guaranteed to them "the promise of My Father," the gift of power, the presence of the Spirit. The other Gospels mention this guarantee and assurance only as the brief final word of His life on earth; but John corrects this impression, and describes this promise and guarantee at length as an important part of the teaching of Jesus on the night before His trial.

At the moment this teaching escaped the disciples. Like Jesus' earlier references to His coming death, they failed to comprehend it. Now the time had come when their minds were to be opened, and they should understand. They had been plunged into depression and despair by the death of the Saviour; and their hopes for the Kingdom of God were crushed. The conviction that He was not dead, as it grew into abiding certainty, rekindled the hope, but produced no understanding; and they still so utterly misconceived the Kingdom of God as to ask, "Lord, dost Thou at this time restore the Kingdom to Israel?" Their awakening to understand the character of Jesus, His mission and His Kingdom, is described in the second chapter of the Acts. Suddenly they saw and knew, and the knowledge was the presence and the power of the Holy Spirit.

The words in which Peter addressed the assembly are the best account of the marvellous experience. Such words, if remembered at all, would be better remembered than the accompanying circumstances (which are liable to be modified by popular belief); and they have a simplicity, directness and impressiveness that compels and ensures remembrance. The quotation from Joel could not be forgotten: it struck the key-note of the incident, and gave the tone which ruled in the development of the young Church. The speech made history and was remembered in history, not indeed verbatim, but in outline and in spirit. This brief outline of an epoch-making address, delivered on a memorable occasion, stands in history as the first utterance of the new Church; and as such is a document of the highest interest. We confine our attention at present to the opening part of this speech.

What Peter lays stress upon is the gift of prophecy which had been suddenly bestowed, i.e., the gift of insight into the development of history, and the Divine, eternal principles that control the movement of events. The disciples perceived now the meaning and purpose embodied in the life and death of the Saviour, to which they had as yet been blind. Jesus had hitherto been above and beyond them, a figure whom they revered and after a dim fashion believed in, but whose teaching and work lay outside the range of their minds. Now they were inspired with His spirit; each of them realized that Jesus was for himself individually the Saviour; and the knowledge was the Spirit and the Power of God. This inspiration was universal, without distinction of sex or rank.

Slavemen and slavewomen, young and old, sons and daughters, all shared alike in it. It is the same principle that Paul states: "There can be neither Jew nor Greek, there can be neither bond nor free, there can be no male and female; for ye are all one in Christ Jesus".

Luke, who more than any other writer in the New Testament notices the part played by women, does not allude to their presence here (unless that is implied in the first verse). The inner meaning of universal inspiration and equality without sex-distinction, which Peter perceived in the scene, was not yet fully realized in the Christian society as it actually was. The Church was not then, and could not for many centuries become, fully dominant within its own house. Underneath the existing form Peter saw what it should be and what it would hereafter be. So did Paul in the words which we have quoted; yet while Paul foresaw the absolute equality that should rule in the perfect Church, he saw also the practical facts of the moment, and he declared that, in the existing state of society inside and outside of the Church, it was not right that women should speak in the public assembly. We must not, therefore, infer from Peter's insight into the ideal future that the actual Church tried to reach the ideal at the moment, or that Peter thought it should make the attempt.

There is always in this world a great gap between the perfect ideal and the possible actuality.

Such is the inner spirit of the event. What were the outward features and facts as they were evident to the disciples and as they appeared to spectators? Two general principles may be laid down in interpreting such a situation. (1) So mighty a change in the mind and powers of individuals does not occur without some remarkable external effects. But (2) the very nature of these effects would prevent their making a clear and uniform impression on those concerned. Had the men who were present recorded separately on that same day their impressions of the physical features of the scene, they would certainly have differed widely.

We have before us two accounts of the scene: that stated by Peter at the moment in his speech, and that derived by Luke from the general belief prevalent in the Church at Jerusalem nearly thirty years after the event. They differ notably. Peter brushes aside the external features as unimportant, fastens on the inner meaning, and dwells on this alone. Yet he shows unmistakably that he was aware of the strange external features which Luke in his narrative dwells upon. The spectators saw these alone: they could not look beneath the surface to the soul: they derided the strange appearance of the scene. Peter acknowledges those features in a word, and passes from them: "These persons are not drunken, as ye suppose; but this is what Joel has foreseen and described".

The Divine influence affects different human beings in different ways. To some it was at that moment overpowering and confusing. To Peter it was on the instant illuminative and strengthening, as it soon became to all. Hitherto he had been a listener and an observer, making sometimes a short statement, and that not always a right or a wise one. Now he could preach an extempore discourse, full of insight and power.

Some or many of the others could only "speak with tongues". In this place we cannot go into the precise meaning of this much-discussed expression. It is sufficient to note that: (1) the gift of tongues was recognized generally in the early Church as one of the forms in which the Divine Spirit manifested itself to give power to the minds of men.

(2) The Apostle Paul does not rank it very high among these forms, but says that it is more advantageous for the individual who received the gift than for the Church in which he used it.

(3) Paul regarded the utterances of this gift as obscure, needing interpretation, "for no man understandeth," and as spoken "not unto men, but unto

God ". Hence, while the devout interpreted the words spoken with tongues on this occasion each in his native language, others regarded them as the babbling of men filled with new wine. Peter rightly disregarded these external signs, visible and audible, and went direct to the spiritual meaning that lay beneath them. Those accompaniments are interesting in themselves, and are in some ways an instructive study; but here, where attention has to be directed only to what is most important, they must be passed in silence.

John tells that Jesus had foretold this gift of the Spirit: "I will pray the Father, and He shall give you another Comforter, that He may be with you for ever, even the Spirit of truth" (xiv. 16 f.). Such was the spiritual truth of this scene. Its external features are described by Luke: "there appeared tongues as of fire, distributing themselves among them; and it sat upon each one of them". But he does not omit the inner truth: "they were all filled with the Holy Spirit".

III

THE BIRTH OF THE CHURCH

Acts ii. 22-47

THE rest of Peter's speech has an imperishable interest, for it is the first statement of the Gospel as understood by the primitive Christians in Jerusalem when they were entering on the work, with which they had been charged, of conveying the Divine message to the world. Luke fully appreciated its historic importance; and the right understanding of it is the key to the whole plan of his history. Luke thought that Peter as yet did not comprehend the full import of the work with which the Church was charged. New situations would arise, and new ideas would be forced on him. This speech states the platform upon which he and the Church started.

After the appeal, "Ye men of Israel, hear these words," the key-note is struck at once, " Jesus the Nazarene ". He is called by the designation which was best known to the audience, and by which they would most surely identify the person intended. It was the designation placed on the cross. It was the designation used by the accusers of Stephen, and by Paul in addressing Agrippa. It was the designation by which Jesus defined himself to Paul, when he appeared to him nigh unto Damascus. It was, in short, the designation by which his enemies described him, and Peter is addressing enemies.

In the speech five facts are stated emphatically. (1) The Divine power had proved itself in and through the person of Jesus by "mighty works and wonders and signs". This is taken as an acknowledged fact; and, since Peter's appeal proved successful, we must understand that his hearers, although opponents, admitted the fact.

(2) The Jews crucified Him through the agency of men outside the law, that is, of Romans.

(3) This took place as part of the plan formed beforehand with full knowledge by God.

(4) Death had no power over Jesus.

(5) David had foretold that He would be raised up.

This address shows what a revolution had taken place in the disciples' views. A few days ago they had been looking for the immediate restoration of the kingdom to Israel. Now they regarded the crucifixion and its shame as the central idea in the salvation planned by God and prophesied by David. They now understood the Divine purpose.

The address was admirably suited to the audience of Jews, to whom the outlook of the Church was still confined. Even the elaborate argument under the fifth heading, which to us may seem far-fetched and inconclusive, was to the Jews probably the most effective of all. Its meaning may be thus expressed: David says, "I shall not be subject to death"; but David died, and we know his tomb, therefore he was not speaking of his individual self, but of his promised offspring, the Messiah; and as was the Jewish custom, he identifies his remote descendant with himself. Now Jesus, his descendant, was not subject to death, but, as you know, He rose. Therefore Jesus is the Messiah. This reasoning was conclusive to the people in Jerusalem who knew the recent facts, and who admitted the argument from prophecy. To a wider audience of strangers and pagans it would not have appealed. We are here within the horizon of Judaism and Jerusalem, and, so to say, under the shadow of the cross. The facts are assumed and admitted by speaker and hearers.

The address pierced the hearers' hearts, and they asked, "What shall we do?" The steps they should take were marked out by Peter: (1) Repentance: the same message as that of John the Baptist.

(2) Baptism in the name of Jesus Christ, that is, with acknowledgment that Jesus is the Christ.

(3) Forgiveness of sins thereby produced.

(4) Divine inspiration, which follows, raising them to the level of the Church and the disciples.

There was, evidently, in the mind of Peter and the disciples a conception of the little Church of Jerusalem gradually widening itself to include the Jewish people; this Jewish Church has its religious centre in the temple, but adds to the duties of the temple the religion of the home. What, then, has become of the command to preach the Gospel to the whole world? Peter has not forgotten this. He alludes to it when he says, " To you is the promise, and to your children, and to all that are afar off, even as many as the Lord our God shall call ". Clearly, Peter understands that those who are afar off—that is, the Gentiles—are to be brought into the Jewish fold; the Jewish nation shall be widened to admit such as are called, who are willing to accept the temple as the national sanctuary and conform to the whole Jewish law. The atmosphere of the passage is still Jewish. The new Church is a sect of the Jews, knit together in wonderful unity and fellowship by the rite of the breaking of bread, and prayers in the house and in the assembly, but accepting the entire Jewish law and ritual with those Christian rites superadded.

The " breaking of bread," so often alluded to by Luke, is undoubtedly an act of religion. It is an accompaniment of the meal in the house: the bread was broken and divided to all as a symbol that all were parts of one whole, one fellowship, one Church, one Master. The common meal was thus a bond of union among the brotherhood, and the young Church aimed at encouraging this union in every way—amongst others, by carrying charity to such a pitch that they regarded their property as common, and people used to sell their possessions and divide them to all according to their varying needs.

But no rule of selling is here stated; in the exact translation a habit arising from love and brotherly kindness is implied, not a regulation enforced on the members. Where property has all ceased to exist, because all has been divided up, there can be no charity. Now the giving of charity according to one's property was one of the most marked features of the early Church. Luke is here describing very generous charity, but not a rule of common property.

In this way the infant Church went on increasing, and in the last verse a process is summed up which may have lasted over many months, until a new stage in the development of the Church began.

IV

THE POWER OF FAITH

Acts III. 1-26

As we have already seen, these first Christians in Jerusalem maintained the Jewish ritual, and to them, as to the other Jews, the temple was the place for the public service of prayer. During this attendance at the temple occurred the striking incident described in Chapter III, the healing of a man, lame from birth, familiar to all visitors at the temple as a beggar, whose station was by the Beautiful Gate.

Pity for human suffering—physical suffering as well as moral—was a marked feature of Jesus' teaching; and probably the aspect of His work which most powerfully touched the hearts of the men among whom He moved, was the sympathy which He showed for their physical suffering. This compassion showed itself especially in medical attention to the sick. The universal experience of missionaries in modern times corroborates this observation: in mission work no avenue leads more directly to the popular heart than the relief of disease and physical pain. It is therefore natural that an incident such as this one should be still living in the memory of the poor Christians of Palestine when Luke was there in A.D. 57-59.

The incident was of the nature of a faith-cure. As the accepted custom among ancient writers prevented Luke from stating exactly the evidence on which he relies, we cannot treat the cure as scientifically attested, nor have we the means of judging how far it was explicable as an ordinary phenomenon of medical practice working on the emotions and the belief. But the story is so lifelike and so circumstantial that its general features cannot be doubted by an unprejudiced mind; and the important consequences that ensued helped to preserve it fresh in the popular memory, and obtained for it a place in Luke's brief history, where only important things are noticed.

It has been doubted whether the faith by which the cure was effected was the faith of the man himself, or of the two Apostles. Surely there should be no doubt. There must have been faith on his part, for without that he could not be cured In Luke VII. 50 the sinner was saved by her faith in Luke VIII. 48 the sufferer was made whole by her faith. But there was also faith on the part of Peter and John. Without that also nothing was possible; and Peter lays special stress on this in his address to the multitude. The cure had been wrought, not by the power of the Apostles, but "in the name of Jesus Christ the Nazarene," that is to say, by their faith in Him. Where Jesus effected a cure, faith was needed only on the one side. Where one of His followers effected a cure, faith on both sides was needed: such was the normal condition, and there is nothing to suggest that this case was exceptional.

It lies also in the imperfect nature of Oriental popular tradition as historical authority, that we get from Luke a very imperfect idea of the lapse of time. It is not made clear at this stage whether weeks or months or years had passed since Pentecost. Luke himself evidently either had no knowledge on this point, or was not interested in it. Time was of little importance to him: the stages in the development of the Church filled his thought, and chronology passed out of his sight and mind, except that, after the fashion of many ancient historians, he at intervals gives some indication of time, and leaves the reader to distribute the intermediate events within the period. Such an indication occurs later, in Chapter XII; and thus we gather that the cure of the lame man took place not very many months after the first Pentecost.

Peter's speech on this occasion marks a distinct advance in thought and philosophic power from that which he made at Pentecost. There is clearly apparent here the historian's intention to indicate by means of these speeches the gradual development of view in the Church, whose standard is that of its leader, Peter. In the former speech the way of salvation was described as consisting of three steps: repentance, baptism, remission of sins; but the connexion between these steps, the moral fact in the man which makes these three steps into one process, was not stated. Now the nature of this process is better understood and set forth in definite words by Peter. The idea of Faith is fundamental in this address. Through Faith comes healing.

May we not believe that the advance in Peter's thought took place through the ennobling influence of the remarkable incident? The consciousness of power brought the consciousness of knowledge: the two are different sides of one mental fact. The intense pity and desire to help gave Peter the power. As soon as the power was exerted, he knew how it acted, and on the instant he said to the spectators that this was not done by the Apostles' power or pity, but that the name of Jesus by faith in His name had effected the cure. Then he stated again the lesson as to the way through repentance and remission of sins, omitting now the ceremony of baptism as external and less important, but adding the inner and vital fact that the issue for the converts will be seasons of refreshing—that is, revival —in which the Divine power should be shown on them and in them.

But even yet Peter has not lost the dream or hope of a restoration of the Kingdom in Palestine: the consummation shall be the sending of the Messiah among them. This Messiah, however, is the same Jesus whom they slew and who has returned to heaven. It is implied that the Kingdom of the Messiah shall be a local one, with Jerusalem and the temple as its centre. A consciousness of the widening of the Kingdom appears only in verse 26, "unto you first,"—that is, to Jews first and afterward to all men is the Servant of God sent. The conception of the Divine plan and purpose is still imperfect in these speeches; but Peter and the Church with him were gradually awakening to fuller consciousness.

The fixed earnest gaze of Peter and John on the lame man, and of the wondering crowd on the Apostles, are noteworthy traits. The soul speaks best through the eyes; and this earnest gaze is often mentioned in Acts as indicative of a certain lofty excitation of the whole inner nature. Wherever, for example, it is mentioned that Paul "fixed his eyes" on some one (as on Bar-Jesus), this power of the mind expressed itself through the eyes.

V

THE SOURCE OF POWER

Acts iv. 1-31

WHILE Peter and John were addressing the people, the Jewish priests and rulers arrested them, and on the morrow arraigned them before a hastily convened council. The Roman masters of the city had no part in this act. They interfered in case of serious disturbance, but generally left to the Jewish rulers the task of preserving order in the precincts of the temple. It was the policy of the high priests to prevent riots, which might attract Roman attention and lead to the curtailment of such powers as the Romans still left to them.

The marvellously vivid picture which Luke gives of this council shows the rulers as at first quite ignorant that the prisoners had been connected with Jesus. Yesterday they had observed the signs of excitement among the people, and taken immediate steps to check it. The question addressed to the prisoners reveals the suspicion that the remarkable cure—an undeniable fact, evident in the patient who stood before the court as a witness—had been produced by unholy and magical arts. If this were established, the case, as being a religious one, fell entirely under their jurisdiction. Peter took the lead in replying, pointing to Jesus as the one and only source of such power as they had exerted, charging their judges with His murder, and drawing the inference that their malice had only served to illuminate His glory.

This answer, so quiet, so restrained, so complete, was conclusive. There was nothing more to do. The intention of the Jewish administration—a perfectly right and wise intention—to nip in the bud a dangerous popular movement, which might lead to conspiracy, disorder, rebellion and bloodshed, was brought to naught by the simple fact that here was neither revolutionary tendency nor trace of conspiracy nor encouragement to rebellion, but only the most peaceable and orderly beneficence. They could not venture to inflict punishment for the mere cure of a sick man, without putting themselves hopelessly in the wrong and rousing public excitement and indignation. Nor could they even venture to take notice of the historical statement and the theory of prophetic fulfilment set forth by Peter. It was safest to let the past remain undisturbed. If controversy about Jesus began, feeling might be roused, the disorder which they dreaded might ensue, and the blame would rest with themselves. From their point of view the less said about the Messiah the better. They therefore instructed the prisoners to say nothing more about Jesus; and even when Peter declared that "we cannot but speak the things which we saw and heard," they merely threatened to punish the two prisoners in case of disobedience, and let them go.

The priests and rulers were taken aback in this inquiry, when they perceived that Peter and John had been with Jesus. They had fancied that with the death of the leader the movement would quiet down, and His followers, peasants devoid of education, would be powerless; and so it had seemed for a time to be. Now suddenly it was made clear to them that those followers could boldly face the national authorities, and speak with ease and power; that without any professional training they could reason convincingly on points of the religious law. It is to this new power that Luke refers when he describes Peter in the court as "filled with the Holy Spirit," possessed and inspired with the Divine power. The Jewish leaders recognized here, and we must recognize, that there was no other explanation of the facts except the influence of Jesus, His inspiration and His continued presence with His followers. What an education those poor peasants and fishermen had enjoyed in constant intercourse with Jesus during His life, and in the consciousness which they now had that He was always with them, even unto the end of the world!

We recognize also that the Divine truth always works in calm and quiet power; it is never hysterical, excited, or violent. What dignity, what self-restraint, what instinctive perception how far to go and where to stop, do Peter and John show here! Nothing can be added and nothing taken away, without impairing the effect. What a contrast between these men and other Jews who had on other occasions proclaimed the Messiah! All those others had been true patriots, devoted, unselfish, ready to die for their belief; but they were hysterical and violent, and their action could only produce rebellion on the Jewish side and stern repression on the part of the Romans. Their enterprises had all been evanescent. This new movement was permanent, because it was quiet, orderly and peaceful. Its followers respected their neighbours and their magistrates, because they respected themselves. This is the touchstone to distinguish the wrong (even when it has an element of right mixed up in its composition) from the right which is Divine.

So ended the first collision between the young Church and the Jewish authorities. The result

was to strengthen the whole congregation, to fill
them with the consciousness of the power that
had been granted them, and to give them confidence
for the future. The event lived in the memory of
the Christians, partly from the picturesque and impressive nature of the facts, partly because it was
the first public exertion of their common power,
and partly because it inaugurated the long series of
contests between the Church and the Jewish rulers.

We can gather in a vague way some idea here
of the lapse of time since the Crucifixion. A certain
interval separated the two events, for the priests
and rulers had no longer fresh in their minds the
memory of Jesus; and it was only when Peter
recalled His death at their hands that they began to
connect the two Apostles with that Teacher whom
they had slain. This seems to require that a
good many months had elapsed, during which the
Church, though making steady progress, had not
attracted the notice of the Jewish administration,
but had appeared to be merely one of those associations which from time to time arose and remained
within the limits of the Hebrew religion. The
orderly behaviour of the Christians, and their use of
the temple as their centre, tended to keep them
safe and obscure. On the other hand, it is not
allowable to suppose that a very long interval had
passed since the death of Jesus, for a Church

V. THE SOURCE OF POWER

containing so many thousands even of quiet, peaceable citizens was likely to be forced into prominence; and this took place through the incident of the lame man. The Jewish leaders were evidently afraid that any talking about Jesus might rouse the populace, and this implies that the memory had not died away, but was comparatively fresh.

VI

THOU SHALT NOT WRONG GOD[1]

Acts IV. 32–v. 11

AT this point Luke again reviews the character of the early Church. We may, perhaps, infer that this second review implies a considerable lapse of time since the first review (II. 44 f); but it must always be remembered that Luke lays little stress on mere considerations of time. He counts according to the steps in the progress of the Church, and the review is made at this point because an important development now occurred in Church administration.

This second review of the early Christians is similar to the first, but adds a new element. Strict translation of the Greek words is here necessary; and loose translation has sometimes produced serious misconception of the meaning. No universal selling of property is mentioned, and no

[1] The title is an early Christian formula, used upon old Phrygian gravestones.

general instructions were issued that members of the Church ought to distribute to the poor all that they possessed. But many of the owners of property ("as many as were possessors of lands or houses"), of their own free will, from love of the brethren, used from time to time to sell their property and bring the proceeds to the Apostles. They acquired merit and honour by these acts of self-sacrifice; and two examples are given, one honest and meritorious, one dishonest and disgraceful.

No such examples would be needed, and no special merit would be acquired, if it had been a principle in the early Church to renounce all private property and give everything to the Church. Peter says in v. 4 that the selling was voluntary, and the money received from the sale was the property of the possessor to employ as he pleased. Nor is it implied that owners of property sold all and reduced themselves to poverty. On the contrary it is stated that none were in want, since the charity of the richer Christians provided for the poorer. A form of charity which swelled the number of the destitute by producing a large number of voluntary paupers, would be inconsistent with the spirit of the narrative. Luke believed with all his heart that such generous charity was right; he lays strong enphasis on the frequency of such acts of sacrifice in the early Church, when the Spirit was moving the hearts of the brethren, and he has the intention of stimulating to similar action the Christians of his own time. But his emphasis is so strong as to have caused misunderstanding of his meaning, as if universal sale of property and the absolute rule of community of goods were carried out in the early Church.

A progress in method is here described. Formerly, when the rich sold their property they used to distribute to the poor themselves (II. 45). Now, as numbers had increased and it was more difficult to know the needs of each, the sellers began to give the proceeds of the sales to form a Church fund, which was regulated and distributed by the Apostles, " as any one had need ". Here we have the beginnings of Church organization. As soon as a permanent fund came into existence, some administration of it was needed; and just as the Apostles took the lead in teaching, so they, as the friends of the Lord and leaders of the brethren, were trusted to manage the fund and distribute the charity. The development of organization implies increased coherence and definiteness in the Church. It was no longer a mere assembly of separate individuals, each acting as the Spirit moved him; it was now becoming a **unified organism** with an administration.

VI. THOU SHALT NOT WRONG GOD

At this point, also, a new figure is introduced on the stage of early Christian history, the first who is named outside the number of those who had known the Saviour personally (I. 21 f.), and one who was destined to play a conspicuous part in the development of the Church, a Levite from Cyprus, Joseph Barnabas. It is an interesting fact that the explanation which is given of his surname is linguistically not correct; but this wrong interpretation, "the son of exhortation," was a popular etymology, which Luke heard current among the people. Popular etymology is commonly unscientific.

The story of Ananias and Sapphira, which follows, is one of the most impressive in this history. It bears strongly marked on it the character of popular belief current in the early Church, and one feels no doubt that Luke heard it in Cæsarea or Jerusalem among the brethren in A.D. 57-59. The members of the young congregation were not all honest and true. The vain desire to gain honour and praise from their associates, impelled some to contribute to the fund; but this lower motive could not make them sincere and whole-hearted in their conduct. A type of this class is exposed in the married pair, who, having sold a piece of land, offered part of the price to the Apostles. The presentation evidently took place publicly at an assembly of the congregation; and the story is told in such a way as to show how the awe-struck brethren gradually came to comprehend the nature of the facts as they occurred. The whole circumstances are not explained at the outset. The reader learns them piece-meal, as the spectators learned them. Such an account is clearly marked as resting on eye-witness; we have a real occurrence remembered and described as it happened. The Church now consisted of thousands, and there were too many members for each to know the other personally. The spectators thought at first that the action of Ananias was as honest as that of Barnabas; and they were struck with panic as the judgment fell on him at Peter's denunciation.

But what a contrast is there between the power which Jesus showed to draw out the best in the nature of those who came into personal relations with Him, and the power which in the presence and aspect of Peter punished the evil as by a stroke of lightning! What a contrast between the unvarying beneficence of Christ's action towards men, and the destroying power which in several cases goes out from the Apostles! Here we feel ourselves in a different atmosphere and a new era; the age of the Gospels is ended; the age of punishments has begun. In the world the practical fact is that, when ordinary government fails to make its subjects act rightly, punishment must be resorted to. Jesus did not need to apply punishment to men; but no very long time had elapsed after He left the Church to govern itself, when the death penalty was foretold and carried out in its assembly. Jesus ruled by love; but now "great fear came upon the whole Church". Yet with some people "the fear of the Lord is the beginning of wisdom".

In the memory of the early Christians the incident survived, because it impressed on them the punishing authority with which the Apostles were invested in the last resort. Peter is not said to have himself exercised the power and inflicted the penalty: he merely denounces the crime and predicts the punishment. But the practical effect is the same: to foresee and denounce is to punish.

The early tradition laid stress chiefly on the moral, and it is characteristic of tradition that features not essential to the moral are omitted, and the circumstances group themselves in the popular memory in such a way as to impart terrific impressiveness to the lesson. Hence some of the facts mentioned in this case are rather hazy because of the omission of others—in marked contrast to the precise details given about the lame man in Chapter IV, his age, his situation, etc.

Ananias is not described as a foreign Jew, like

Barnabas, but we cannot think that he lived and owned property in Jerusalem. In the publicity of life in those regions, the price of a property would be known to all, even to many who did not know the owner personally. Yet the narrative seems to suggest that Peter became aware of the hidden crime through special insight. Had the price been widely known, Ananias, who was perfectly free to use the money as he chose, could hardly have seriously intended to maintain the pretence of offering the whole price. Probably, therefore, he was a foreign Jew. Were the circumstances fully recorded, this and some other difficulties in understanding the exact facts would probably disappear. For us here it is sufficient to observe that the intention of the narrative is to burn deep on the popular conscience a moral warning, and not merely to record the precise details of a historical event. It is a moral apologue, not as invented to embody a moral, but as remembered because it did so.

VII

THE TEST OF TRUTH

Acts v. 12-42

AGAIN a certain interval, which cannot be estimated exactly, elapsed before the next incident in the history of the Church. As in Chapter IV, this new incident arose through the enmity of the Sadducees (to whom the chief priests belonged, while the humbler priests were generally Pharisees: VI. 7). On the other hand the Pharisees, who had been so hostile to Jesus himself, do not at this time appear as enemies of the young Church; and one of the leading Pharisees actually spoke in its defence at the trial which now occurred.

Their comparative friendliness to the first Christians for a time contrasts strongly with their fanatical hatred of Jesus, and arose from the Judaic character of the Church at this stage, when it had the Temple as its centre and sanctuary. The Pharisees were nationalists and patriots, and regarded the Church as a sect of the nation, which added to the

Jewish ritual some unessential and private features, while it continued true to the essential facts of Hebraism. The Sadducees had their eyes fixed on the Roman officers, and were apprehensive lest anything should rouse Jewish national feeling and cause trouble with their Roman masters. The Pharisees had an affection for all who showed strong national and religious feeling and who made the Temple their haunt. The Sadducees dreaded the very name Messiah, and forbade it to be mentioned. The Pharisees loved the name, though they had hated the One whom they considered a false Messiah: they knew that the Apostles were followers of Him whom they had hated so, but apparently they thought that the followers had abandoned the more objectionable features of their Master's teaching, especially the placing of Gentiles on an equality of rights with Jews. Moreover, the Sadducees hated and disbelieved the doctrine of a future life, and the Apostles were preaching the Resurrection (IV. 2).

The first trial had ended in a mere warning to the Apostles not to preach. They were now arrested for preaching in spite of the prohibition. During the night they escaped from prison; and in the morning they were found actually preaching inside the Temple. Hitherto they had preached only in the Portico of Solomon on the eastern side of the Temple, or in a private house. To preach inside the Temple was a bolder act, especially for escaped prisoners. The manner of their escape is not described in detail: a "messenger (angelos) of the Lord" is a term that covers any one who announces or carries into effect the will of God. That Luke regarded the escape as effected by supernatural agency might at first seem clear, and this will be enough for most readers. Those who inquire more minutely will recognize both that the narrative has passed from the Semitic to the Greek mind (for Luke was a Greek), and that in other cases (e.g. XIV. 20, XX. 9 f., XXVIII. 3), as we shall see, Luke's statement of the facts does not necessitate (and in the last case forbids) the intervention of supernatural agency, though he himself was perhaps inclined to regard them all as proofs of supernatural power. But in no case does he say that supernatural influence was brought into play: he merely states the facts as he had learned them, and leaves the reader to judge of their nature.

Here we must observe that the people and the rulers, who had all been so much impressed by the cure of the lame man, took no notice of the escape from prison. They therefore saw nothing supernatural in it; and when one thinks of the very simple character of Eastern prisons in modern times and of the way in which prisoners are often

allowed out by the gaolers on parole, one sees that
in this case probably some Semitic popular fashion
of stating a fact whose exact nature was not remembered
has passed into the language of Luke from
the mouth of his informants in Palestine.

The Apostles in the Temple were again arrested,
but in a courteous way, " without violence ". They
were now so much respected by the populace, that
any violence offered to them before a large concourse
might have caused a riot, which it was the object
of the Sadducee rulers to avoid. This political
aspect of the conduct of the ruling priests is never
mentioned in the tradition, which remembered
matters of doctrine (as in IV. 2), but disregarded
political facts. In the second half of Acts it is a
marked feature that relations with the State are
stated so precisely by Luke from his own observation:
in the first half they are rarely thought of,
because the popular mind and tradition in Jerusalem
did not observe or remember them.

In answering the charge of disobedience to the
former orders of the Council, Peter repeated boldly
the Apostles' message, and emphasized their resolve
to "obey God rather than men". The constant
reiteration of this message was now threatening to
produce in the people the belief that Jesus had
been unjustly slain; and as the Apostles cast on
the Jewish leaders the responsibility for His murder,

the people might take vengeance on the guilty ones. The rulers thought that the Apostles "intended to bring this Man's blood upon them". Peter's bold defiance began to suggest to their minds that the safest way might be to kill the Apostles and prevent the danger; but they could not carry with them the whole Council.

Gamaliel, one of the most famous of all the Rabbis, spoke the mind of the Pharisees, discouraging any strong action and advising that the Christians should be let alone, as the movement would soon exhaust itself if it were caused by mere human power, while if it were the work of God it was both vain and wicked to fight against it. In Gamaliel's speech there probably lay under the surface some move in the partisan strife between Sadducees and Pharisees, which did not interest or impress the memory of the Church His sentiments seemed to the Christians to be a Divine inspiration. They accepted his test of truth, and remembered it in his own impressive words,—"Refrain from these men, and let them alone; for if this counsel or this work be of men, it will be overthrown; but if it is of God, ye will not be able to overthrow them".

Amid this diversity of opinion the rulers could not venture on extreme measures; and they were content to warn the Apostles and to beat them, hoping thus to frighten others from joining the movement.

Notwithstanding the action of the rulers, the Apostles continued steadfast in their duty. They taught daily, both in the Temple and at home. The preaching had begun in a house (II. 2, ff), but from II. 46 onwards it was connected rather with the Temple, especially the Portico of Solomon (v 12). The home was reserved rather for more intimate and private communion among the brethren, when the daily meal was accompanied by the solemn rite of "The Breaking of Bread". But the surroundings are still purely Jewish in appearance. The very slight references to a wider horizon and a wider world for the Gospel are now significantly wanting; and the sympathetic opinion of the Pharisees, which saw in the young Church only a fervently national school of Hebrew thought, seemed to be finding full justification. Yet the seeds of a wider movement were in the soil, destined very soon to waken to life and to appear above the ground.

VIII

GOOD ORDER MAKES FOR ACTIVITY IN THE CHURCH

Acts VI. 1-7

THE distribution of a permanent Church Fund meant an increase of work ; and, after a certain lapse of time (which was probably not long), the Apostles found that this financial task threatened to interfere with the more urgent duty of teaching, while the congregation found that some were overlooked in the daily ministration. Taking together II. 46, IV. 35, VI. 1, 2, we observe a kind of congregational life, in which the funded donations of the rich were used to furnish a daily meal for the poor and especially for the widows, and in which some difference of character and feeling began to exist between two distinct classes, one the Jews of Palestine, the other the Jews belonging to foreign countries. The latter class are usually called Hellenists, because they spoke the Greek or Hellenic language, and were much better educated in the Hellenic civilization than the native Palestinian Jews.

It was inevitable that, as a rule, the native Jews should be better known to the leading persons in the congregation, the Apostles especially, who were originally all natives of Palestine; and there may have been some ground in fact, though not in intention, for the complaint of the Hellenists that their widows were suffering from neglect.

The complaint was promptly met by a further step in organization which the Apostles proposed— the appointment of Seven men to serve the tables. It is not implied that the Apostles previously served, but only that it was now found necessary to have special officials charged with a duty which had hitherto been done in an unregulated and haphazard fashion. Responsibility for the duty must be imposed on some definite persons, and as the Apostles could not undertake the work, the Seven were chosen by the congregation. Hitherto various persons had acted voluntarily, as the need called; and in this way capability had been tested. Those who had most approved themselves and gained the respect and good report of the people were now chosen. They were also men of wisdom who were likely to show tact and good sense in distributing alms suitably among claimants who thought that they had been neglected. The

44 VIII. GOOD ORDER ACTIVATES THE CHURCH

Patriarch Chrysostom in the fourth century says that "it needed great philosophy to bear with the complaints of the widows". This early congregation was, after all, only human, and had its share of faults.

Luke names the Seven, but only two of them appear further in his history. He had good information here at his disposal up to a certain point. In the list he gives no information about any except Stephen, who proved a leader in the Church, and Nicolas, a Greek of Antioch, converted to Judaism and thereafter to Christianity. The statement about Nicolas is evidently intended by Luke to mark the first appearance of a Gentile, originally a heathen, in a leading position among the Christians; and it is important to note that Nicolas was a proselyte, i.e. he had conformed entirely to the Jewish ritual and the requirements of the law. Now it is certain that ordinary Jews would dislike to have their food apportioned and distributed by a Gentile, and we may fairly infer that desire to avoid such difficulties would have prevented the congregation from selecting Nicolas, unless he had some special suitability for a particular sphere of duty. In fact we must infer that other proselytes had joined the Church, and that Nicolas had the duty of looking after them and giving information about their needs. Thus we recognize the growing complexity, as well as the increase in numbers of the Church. We observe also the spirit of fairness that guided the action of the congregation.

If Nicolas represented a special class, probably the others had fixed spheres of duty. We notice in VII. 9 that there were other divisions of Jews in Jerusalem, meeting in their separate synagogues. It may be taken as highly probable that the Church drew its members from all of these synagogues, and that the rest of the Seven were specially qualified to represent particular sections of the people.

The Apostles proposed that there should be Seven. The number was evidently a suitable one; and, as it seems unlikely that the suitability lay merely in its being a sacred number in old Hebrew belief, we must suppose that there were seven obvious spheres of duty. But on this point Luke gives no information. The tradition of the Church preserved the names of the Seven, but was silent about divisions and all such ephemeral matters. The historical scholar may regret the silence, but Luke did not write for modern historians, he wrote for the Christian congregations of his own day, and he recorded what they needed and desired.

The official work imposed on the Seven did not supersede the duty incumbent on all members of the congregation to evangelize. On the contrary, this proof of public confidence stimulated them to more active mission work. One of the qualifications in choosing the Seven had been that they should be full of the Spirit; and now the Church, through improvement in practical organization, took a new start in vigour of spiritual life. A well-governed community is also always an active and energetic community. The next steps in the progress of the Church were made by two of the Seven, and not by any Apostle. It was, doubtless, the facts of subsequent history, and not order of precedence in the election, that makes Luke name Stephen first in the list and Philip second. Church tradition remembered the names in this order. We have here not an official record, but the memory of the Christians in Jerusalem.

Nor should we think that the appointment of the Seven put an end to the voluntary work that had hitherto been done in distributing the public benevolence. That work was now regulated, but did not cease. The congregation at Jerusalem was always poor; and the Church from first to last undertook the charge of the poor, and especially of widows (IX. 41).

IX

THE DEATH OF STEPHEN THE VICTORY OF THE CHURCH

Acts VI. 8–VII. 60

WITH the appointment of the Seven began a period of activity and rapid growth. Especially "a great company of the priests were obedient to the Faith". The lower priests were mainly Pharisees, in contrast to the Sadducee high-priests; and the approximation of the Pharisees to the Church was evidently still continuing. The term "obeyed" is carefully chosen: these priests added the Law of Christ to the strict Hebrew ritual. The Church could still be mistaken for a school or sect of Judaism.

Stephen burst these bonds. He boldly taught that the Temple and the Law of Moses were evanescent, because the Faith of Jesus must recreate the Law and abrogate the exclusive sanctity of the Temple. His teaching roused disputation in several Hellenist[1] synagogues—evidently those

[1] A "Hellenist" was a Jew who had been educated amid Greek surroundings, and spoke Greek as his familiar tongue.

IX. STEPHEN'S DEATH THE CHURCH'S VICTORY

where he, as himself a Hellenist, had chiefly preached.

Now this teaching marks a forward step beyond anything mentioned in Acts previously; but it was a step which the Church made as a whole. Stephen was not disowned by the Apostles, though his teaching was more outspoken than theirs. He was recognized by the Church as uttering the mind and the words of Jesus. His trial followed; and it is described in terms which show the deep veneration felt for him. The analogy between it and the trial of the Lord was clearly brought out in the early tradition; no such analogy appears in the account of the Apostles' trials. Stephen was accused in terms which recall some charges made against Jesus, and false witnesses were employed against both. The violent passions roused and the flagrant injustice of the methods employed mark both trials. There are, however, two differences. Stephen replied. Jesus answered never a word. Stephen was deeply moved. Jesus was perfectly quiet throughout.

The expression "false witnesses" does not imply that they invented words which Stephen had not used, but that they took his isolated sayings apart

A "Hellene" was a Gentile possessed of the Greek education and way of thinking, whether or not he was Greek by blood.

from their context, and thus put into them an unjustified innuendo It was easy to distort his teaching about the incompleteness of the Hebrew Law into blasphemy against Moses and against God; and this was the evidence. The trial, as we notice, originated, not from the Sadducee rulers, nor from the bigoted native Jews, but from the Hellenist synagogues where thought was freer. The Hellenist Jews felt that they themselves had gone exactly to the right point in freedom of thought, and they were enraged against one who went further in the same direction. How the trial might have gone if Stephen had shown a desire to conciliate his opponents, and had stooped to minimize or explain away his views, there is no possibility of conjecturing. He took the opposite course, seizing the opportunity of giving emphasis to his teaching; and his concluding words press home the charge against his opponents with a passionate enthusiasm, which a colder intellect might even call provocative.

His hearers believed that the Law was given to Moses once for all, perfect and final, needing only to be rightly interpreted, and that the Temple was the one chosen Sanctuary where God revealed himself. Stephen argued in his outspoken and individual speech that :—

1. The revelation of God's Will and Covenant had been gradual, and began long before Moses.

2. It had been made, not in the Temple, but in other places and in heathen lands.

3. God's Promise often seemed at the moment to be impossible of fulfilment, yet His Covenant always proved true and ought to be accepted as sufficient in itself as soon as it was made.

4. The Jews at every stage were slow to believe, obstinate enemies and persecutors of those through whom God was working, as Joseph whom they sold into slavery, and Moses whom they cast out in infancy, rejected when he first came to deliver them, and turned away from after he had led them out of Egypt, at the very time when he was receiving God's greatest revelation.

5. At every stage the actions of these rebellious and unbelieving Jews served only to work out God's Will: their treatment of Joseph and Moses placed both in a position to serve the development of the Divine purpose.

6. God appointed a Tabernacle. Solomon built the Temple. God dwells not in a house built by men.

Although Jesus is not mentioned in this review of Hebrew history, He is in the speaker's mind throughout; and the hearers could not fail to draw the hidden reference to Him from every biting sentence. He was rejected, scorned, ill-treated like Joseph and Moses. The Jews had disbelieved the promise made in Him, as they had disbelieved past promises. This meaning was so evident that the audience, judges and witnesses, grew ever more angry; and Stephen must have felt this, for he suddenly broke off the line of his argument and burst into the indignant climax, VII. 51-53, pointing the moral in terms of the most cutting rebuke. The accused became the accuser. He charged them all with the murder of the Prophets and of the Righteous One, and with continual disobedience to the Law in its letter and its spirit.

The speech was interrupted. It had reached its climax, though probably not its conclusion. Stephen's point, that Israel could never obey the Law, was afterwards a favourite Pauline idea. Whether Stephen would have proceeded, as Paul hereafter always did, to argue that the Jews could get through Jesus the righteousness which they could never win from obedience to the Law, remains unknown. The audience was now mad with fury at this open defiance, as Stephen trampled on their deepest prejudices and their pride of race and birth and institutions. At the beginning of his speech they had seen his face glow with enthusiasm, shining as the face of an angel, "reflecting the glory of the Lord" (2 Cor. III. 18), as Paul always remembered it, and had evidently described it to Luke. That sight had produced a deep impression and secured a hearing so far for the speaker, in spite of the dislike for the evident drift of his words. Now the audience could not restrain its rage, and their demonstration stopped the speech.

Stephen, however, was only more transported with enthusiasm and inspiration than before. As he had begun by mentioning "the God of the Glory," so now he beheld the Glory itself. His gaze pierced into the very Heaven. Time and human limitations were effaced for him, and he beheld the real, the eternal truth, "the Glory of God, and Jesus standing on His right hand".

Those who set store by details in the emblematic expression of Divine facts as the feeble language of man seeks to describe them, may find either some significance or some inconsistency in the fact that Jesus is elsewhere pictured as sitting at the right hand of God. To us such differences seem to proceed from the weakness of human language in the picturing of Divine realities.

The catastrophe followed immediately. The assembly burst through all the restraints of Roman law and order, but it is noteworthy that they observed all the forms of the Jewish Law in giving to the murder of Stephen the appearance of a judicial execution. It is not improbable that a form of sentence was pronounced, in which Paul gave his vote. Stephen was, according to the Law, taken outside the camp (Lev. XXIV. 14 ff.); the witnesses cast the first stone at him (Deut. XVII. 7), preparing for the active work by taking off their upper garments and giving them in charge to Saul, who was evidently placed in charge of the whole proceedings.

One effect of the explosion seems to have been to destroy the *rapprochement* between the Pharisees and the young Church. Stephen had made it evident that the Church was not a mere school of Judaism, and his teaching had been accepted by all. A persecution followed on the moment, and it is described as breaking out in full fury even before Stephen was buried The Christians fled to all parts of Judea and Samaria, and it seemed for a moment that the Church in Jerusalem was killed. But the words of Stephen proved true: it was always the acts of the Jews in resisting and rejecting the Prophets that became the means of effecting the Divine purpose. He had made a deep impression by his life, he made a far deeper impression by his death.

Stephen was buried by "devout men". This term [1] might include any that worshipped the God of the Hebrews, the one true God. The employment of such a term in this case suggests the probability that strangers buried Stephen, while the Christians were hunted, and could take no action themselves.

[1] A different Greek word from XVII. 17. see footnote, Section XVIII.

X

TRUE AND FALSE BELIEF

Acts VIII. 1-24

THE most striking result of the severe persecution that began at Jerusalem after the murder of Stephen—the result which stood out clearly and firmly fixed in the memory of the Church and so passed into the record of Luke—was that the new teaching, hitherto confined to Jerusalem, was now carried widely through Palestine, inasmuch as "they that were scattered abroad passed through (the country) spreading the good news of the Word," town by town and village by village. The congregation in Jerusalem had become very numerous, and thousands of missionaries were now going about, each working in his own way, conversing in the guest-houses where they were received, telling the news of the capital to the rustics in the villages, or formally preaching the Word. Not a single detail concerning the Jewish part of the land is recorded at this point. Luke contents himself with the general statement, giving us to understand that a strong impression was produced throughout the Jewish towns and villages.

The historian's interest is now directed to the next stage in the growth of the Church, viz. the spread of the new Faith to non-Jewish peoples and regions. The mere diffusion of the Word among Jews alone would have tended to confine the Church within the narrower form of a mere sect of the Hebrews, as it had at first appeared to be in Jerusalem. That stage has already been sufficiently described; and Luke goes on now to depict the process whereby the Faith spread to the Samaritans, the Phœnicians (XI. 19, XV. 2), and northern Syria generally (IX. 2, XI. 19). In all those regions, except perhaps Samaria, there were many Jews; and it was natural that the fugitives from Jerusalem, being almost all Jews by race, should come most quickly and easily into relations with their own nation. Thus most of them confined their work within the circle of the Jewish assembly in each town. Some, however, did not thus limit their efforts; and it is to this class of missionaries that Luke now directs the attention of his readers.

The first step beyond the circle of the Synagogue —i.e. the Jews and proselytes—in each town, was taken by Philip, one of the Seven, who went down to Samaria and proclaimed the Messiah and the

X. TRUE AND FALSE BELIEF

Kingdom of God to its inhabitants. No special reason is given for this step. No special command or revelation to Philip is mentioned: and we are left to infer that it arose through his own initiative in the general scattering of the brethren. Nor is it stated what special meaning he gave to the Kingdom of God; but it is noteworthy that this term has not been mentioned in the early preaching at Jerusalem since the question of i. 6, which shows such a misapprehension of its real nature; and it is probable that a step in the method and the scope of Christian teaching is implied to have been made by Philip.

The importance of Philip's action lay mainly in the fact that the Samaritans, though partly of Jewish blood, were schismatics, who were hated and despised by the Jews because they claimed to possess among themselves the true Temple and the true Law, whereas the Jews held them to be mere pretenders and heretics, worse than aliens. The Samaritans believed in and were waiting for the coming of the Messiah, and it was probably through this expectation on their part that Philip was led on to preach the true Messiah and His Kingdom to them; and he doubtless remembered the conduct of Jesus to the woman of Samaria.

Among those who thus were brought into the Church was a man named Simon, one of a class of persons very numerous in that age. He was teacher of a kind of philosophic religion, in which the Divine Nature was described as manifesting itself in various degrees of intensity to mankind, and embodying itself in certain individuals with greater or less gradations of power. There was a certain higher side to this thought: it concerned itself with the power of God and it recognized as a fundamental fact that God took an interest in mankind and revealed himself to men. But Simon, while not unconscious of this higher side, practised on the credulity and superstition of the multitude. He pretended that he was the most complete impersonation of God's power, and he was accepted by the whole people on his own pretension as that power of God (i.e. that embodiment of Divine power) which is entitled "Great". This claim he supported by performing sorceries, which deluded the populace.

From similar cases which are known at that time we can imagine what sort of arts Simon practised. Partly he had some scientific knowledge and some command over the resources of nature through chemical and other processes. Partly he used pure jugglery and legerdemain. Partly he imposed himself on the minds of his audience by clever teaching of a semi-philosophic type.

But it is important to observe that Simon was

not a mere impostor. There was in him an element of belief, and a certain vague perception of truth, as the following considerations show. In this brief history, in which Luke with marvellous skill and insight concentrates attention on the great stages of his subject, there would be no room to tell how the Church proved stronger than a mere vulgar cheat. To relate that were needless and valueless. In every sentence Luke has in mind the interests of the Christian congregation of believers generally, and they did not need to be convinced that a mere impostor could not fight against the sword of the Lord and Philip and Peter and John. The very fact that, when his devotees and dupes deserted him, Simon could not stand out against Philip, but believed and was baptized, shows a certain capacity for appreciating spiritual truth, and a certain power to learn. The man who could accept his defeat and make his conqueror his teacher was not a mere charlatan; nor would Philip have been deceived by a mere impostor.

Although this new step had been made by Philip without formal authorization from the Church and the Twelve, it was regarded with no prejudice by them, but was estimated fairly and dispassionately on its merits. Peter and John, who had taken a leading place in the counsels of the Church, were sent to Samaria to investigate. The one question asked was whether the Spirit of God was in the work. Where the Spirit led, the Church went. This openness and freedom of mind, this readiness to accept new methods and wider views, this willingness to learn and to advance, is a striking feature of the primitive Church.

Evidently the possession of the Spirit is here regarded in simple fashion as indicated through certain external phenomena (as in II 4, x 45). This is an early trait. Luke's informant (as to whom there will be more to say in next Section) faithfully reported to him the primitive view of the Church, that those outward phenomena and acts proved the indwelling Spirit. Afterwards Paul attained and taught the deeper view that the transformation of the individual's moral character and nature, as shown in his life, is the truest test of the possession of the Spirit, and that the external phenomena are, as he says to the Corinthians and everywhere implies, of secondary importance.

Luke in his history is alive to both views. He tells how the Spirit was proved in the Church by the moral character and conduct of the brethren (II. 46, and other places), but he accurately records the primitive view; he always mentions prominently the external proofs of the Spirit, and nowhere describes the situation purely from the more developed point of view of Paul's teaching.

In this respect the history shows itself faithful and true to the actual character of the earliest period.

It is not stated that every Samaritan convert received the Spirit. The Greek words describe a long process: the Apostles were laying hands on them individually, and each then received the Spirit. Simon saw the process, and the imperfection of his belief, the hollowness of his character, and the moral worthlessness of his specious scientific knowledge, were disclosed. He was eager to obtain the same power that the Apostles possessed; and he came offering to purchase it with money, as if it were an education in a scientific process according to formal laws, which could be taught by a professor to his pupils for a fee. That was the only knowledge that he possessed; and his moral nature had not been so far influenced that he had shared his wealth with the poor, or begun to feel ashamed of the gains which he had made by such dubious means.

Peter rebuked him in strong and prophetic terms. The prophecy is concealed in the ordinary translation; the Greek means "thou art for a gall of bitterness and a fetter of unrighteousness," i.e. a cause of bitterness and corruption to others. A man of such powers as Simon possessed must be a cause of much evil in the world, when these powers are guided neither by true moral and religious ideas nor by right knowledge.

His answer brings out his utter failure to apprehend the moral side of true knowledge. Peter had told him that the only way to forgiveness for him was through repentance and prayer. Simon replied by asking the Apostles to pray for him, that he might be spared the misfortunes which Peter had just denounced against him. He still regarded the process of salvation as something external to himself and not affecting his inner life and character. Others must pray for him; persons who possessed more of the Divine power than he possessed must help him. Of real repentance and inward change of heart he shows not a trace. Thus he justifies the doubts that Peter expressed whether he could be forgiven. We must understand that those doubts arose not as to whether forgiveness was possible, but as to whether Simon would repent and earn it.

And so Simon passes out of this history, but not out of the wider life of the Church, which remembered how he had become a leader of error, a root spreading bitterness and evil among the Christians, the first person who taught and obtained credence for a doctrine opposed to that of the Apostles. He continued to claim a place within the Church, and by remaining inside it to increase his power of doing harm. But no early tradition is recorded; only in the second century and later have we any further account of his fortunes; and the tradition had gathered around it, in the long lapse of time, much that is incredible and impossible, so that no single detail can be stated with confidence about him; but the general fact stands out plain that Peter correctly gauged his character and foresaw its consequences.

XI

THE PROPHET IN THE WILDERNESS

Acts VIII. 25-40

FROM Samaria the Apostles returned to Jerusalem, and on the way their cordial approval of the advance which Philip had made was shown by the fact that they occupied themselves in telling the good news of the Gospel in many Samarian villages. Their journey must therefore have been slow. Philip did not return with them, but went away into the wilderness that lay on the south of Judea between Palestine and Egypt. Then followed another incident, one of the most picturesque in the whole book, narrated in a marked style, which is characterized more by the spirit of the Old Testament than by the usual tone of the New.

Philip was ordered by the messenger of the Lord to go southwards into the wilderness to strike the road that leads from Jerusalem to Gaza and thence along the coast towards Egypt and Ethiopia.

XI. THE PROPHET IN THE WILDERNESS

There he saw a traveller, an important Ethiopian official, superintendent of the royal treasury, who had visited Jerusalem to worship and was now returning to his own land. A traveller of such high rank, with a long journey before him not free from danger, was of course accompanied by some considerable retinue of servants and guards. But these are not alluded to; they were of no consequence in this history, which concentrates attention on the important incidents and persons, and leaves the rest out of notice. The Spirit moved Philip to approach this officer and address him. An opportunity was afforded by the book which the Ethiopian was reading aloud to himself: it was the prophecies of Isaiah, and the passage was in the fifty-third chapter, where the prophet describes the Suffering Servant of God in terms which have always been applied to Jesus from the time when His death opened men's eyes to the real character and purpose of His life.

As was natural in that period, when Greek was the language of educated men, the Ethiopian was reading the Greek translation, which sometimes differs considerably from the Hebrew; and the second of the two verses that he recited is so rendered in the Greek as to be obscure and incorrect. It was therefore not strange that the reader, without some one to guide him, found himself unable to comprehend the words, or understand who was described in them. The second verse, Is. LIII. 8, is given after the Hebrew in the Revised Version of the Old Testament thus: "By oppression and judgment (i.e. by an unfair sentence) He was taken away: and as for His generation (i.e. the men of His time), who among them considered that He was cut off out of the land of the living?"

Philip had his opportunity. The door was opened to him. The conclusion of the second verse especially gave him his cue: "for the transgression of My people was He stricken". No other passage in the Old Testament so plainly anticipates the unique career of Jesus, which worked out the ideal of the Messiah in a way utterly different from the expectation of the ordinary Jews. Beginning from this Scripture he expounded to the Ethiopian the purpose and the results of Christ's life on earth. After a time they came to a water by the way; and there Philip baptized the Ethiopian at his own request. Then they parted.

Philip was caught away by the Spirit of the Lord, turning towards the north by the old Philistine city of Ashdod (Azotus), and preaching in all the towns of the coast lands till he came to Cæsarea, the Roman capital of Palestine. This missionary progress probably occupied a considerable time, as there were many towns and villages in this fertile region, and Philip would be likely to do his work thoroughly in each.

In Cæsarea, at last, he settled permanently as head of the Church in that city. There Luke found and conversed with him for several days, when he, with the rest of Paul's companions, landed at Cæsarea on the way to Jerusalem in A.D. 57. There afterwards Luke seems to have spent, in the society of Philip and the Cæsarean Church, the two years that Paul was detained by the procurator Felix in prison. There he met the four daughters of Philip, who, being prophetesses, occupied an influential position in the Church.

In the Acts few persons are mentioned unless they were of real historical importance or concerned in some action which Luke regarded as of critical consequence. So, for example (as will be shown more fully at a later stage), the minute account of the conduct and even the emotions of the slave-girl Rhoda in XII. 13 ff. is not, as some might hastily think, wasted on trifling personal matters that do not concern the growth of the Church. That is Luke's way of mentioning his authority without talking about himself. He had spoken with Rhoda and had heard from her the detailed account which he has transmitted to us; and he intimates thus that he had first-rate authority for the account of a remarkable scene.

So with the prophetesses. Apparently they play no part in this history; but Luke knew that they did play a part. They were his guarantee for a notable episode in his narrative, and a brief consideration of this will throw much light on his method of gathering information, and will show on what trustworthy evidence his statements rest.

In that account of the scene on the road to Gaza, Philip is set before the reader like one of the ancient prophets such as Elijah or Elisha. Every step that he takes is carefully described as suggested by Divine command or inspiration. On the contrary, the Samarian incident, in spite of its importance in the growth of the Church, is not said to have been suggested by Divine command. In Samaria Philip appears only as a subordinate whose action had to be inspected and approved by the superior authority; but in the wilderness he stands forth alone as the hero of the occasion One feels that the difference of tone is due to the fact that the Samarian incident was described to Luke by Philip himself, with a modesty and self-suppression characteristic of his personality. He gave the credit mainly to the Apostles as greater than himself. He would not glory in the revelations made to him. In the same spirit Paul apologizes for once doing so, and explains that it was forced upon him by the attacks to which he had been exposed.[1]

[1] 2 Corinthians XII. 5 ff.

On the other hand, the interview with the Ethiopian is described by an admirer of Philip's, who also was in Luke's estimation an excellent authority. The picture of Philip like a Hebrew prophet suggests that this authority was one or all of Philip's daughters, the prophetesses, who were informants of the highest trustworthiness. Their striking and picturesque account of the incident imprinted itself on his memory, and is reproduced in their Hebrew prophetic style, while he doubtless had Philip's confirmation of the facts.

While the style of narrative varies in the two incidents, the practical range of Philip's action is much the same. The daughters picture their father with loving admiration, but they do not enhance the facts. As at Samaria, he baptizes, but he is not said to convey the Spirit to his convert. The old Hebrew fervour of religious feeling, which animated the prophetesses, saw the hand of God in everything, and described in symbolic language the Divine guidance that was given to Philip at every step. Philip doubtless was not less conscious of the Divine aid in all his work, but he did not speak so openly about it. We have in these two incidents an example of different points of view, arising from Luke's reliance on different authorities; but each part of the narrative makes the other part more distinct. We can understand how the prophetesses would have pictured Philip as the prophet of God pitted against the false prophet Simon, and how Philip might have told simply that he was moved to address the Ethiopian in the chariot. It is not difficult to imagine why it was that Luke's fine literary sense led him to narrate the Samarian events in Philip's own simpler style, and to prefer the impressive picture given by the daughters of the Ethiopian's conversion.

The latter person remains an enigmatical figure. Was he a Jew by blood, born in Ethiopia? or was he an Ethiopian by blood, affected and proselytized by Jewish religious influence? Discoveries made within the last few years show that in the fifth century B.C. there was a colony of Jews settled already for a long time on the south frontier of Egypt where it borders on Ethiopia; and the spread of their influence into that country is thus shown to be natural. Whatever his race, the Ethiopian, as a eunuch, was excluded by the Jewish Law from the assembly of the Lord; and Philip's action is recorded as a proof that no man, however maimed or humiliated, was excluded from the grace of the Saviour. The Ethiopian is nowhere regarded by Luke as an example of the admission of aliens to share in the privileges of the Church, any more than Nicolas of Antioch. Proselytes in the full sense were freely accepted as members of the Church from the beginning.

XII

THE WORK AND POWER OF PETER

Acts IX. 32-43

"PETER went through all parts." Never was a big piece of work mentioned in words so few, yet so complete and comprehensive. The former mission to Samaria was now widened to embrace the whole extent of the growing Church; and the same kind of work which took place in Samaria must undoubtedly be understood to have occurred in every place that Paul visited. His action was not restricted to the cities, as Philip's was (VIII. 40). It included the villages (VIII. 25). It was everywhere. It extended not merely to Judea and Samaria and Galilee (IX. 31), but also to Antioch (Gal. II. 11), to Corinth (Cor. I. 12), and, as we may be sure, much farther.

This is the work of years, probably of a lifetime. It marks out Peter as the great missionary among the older Apostles. It shows why it was part of Peter's duty, in view of an impending persecution, to send to the churches of Asia Minor the Epistle known as 1 Peter. In the prosecution of this great work he could be only seldom in Jerusalem; hence the leadership of the central Church, which lay with him in the earliest years, necessarily passed to other hands; and in later years James appears to have occupied the most prominent position in that congregation (Acts XV. 13, 19; XXI. 18; Gal. II. 9).

A process of world-wide extent and importance like this is summed up in five words; and yet such is the art and historic skill of the narrative that its character stands out clearly before the reader.

Two incidents are selected from an early stage of this process as illustrations of Peter's power. In Luke's estimation these are the most important acts known to him during that long missionary career of Peter; they proved his Divine mission, and they were accepted in proof by the people among whom they were performed. It shows how different is the spirit of the twentieth century from that of the first, that what was then considered by all to be indispensable as a proof of truth now constitutes a difficulty to prevent more general acceptance of truth. Both the incidents are deeds of compassion and healing, similar to the acts recorded of Jesus in the Gospels, and have no resemblance to the acts of judgment and punishment which sometimes occur in Luke's history.

The first incident occurred at Lydda, a large village on the high road from Jerusalem to Cæsarea and to Joppa. In this situation it must naturally have been one of the first places to hear the Gospel from the lips of travellers, and Peter found there a congregation of the saints. Among these was probably Mnason, the ancient disciple in whose house Paul, Luke, and their company lodged (according to the right interpretation) on their way from Cæsarea to Jerusalem; and on our view the mention of his name and early conversion is probably intended to signalize one of the informants from whom Luke derived his knowledge of this incident. In Lydda Aeneas, who had been palsied and bedridden for eight years, was ordered by Peter to rise, "for Jesus Christ healeth thee". There is no allusion here to faith on the part of Aeneas, except that he forthwith obeyed the command. Nor is it stated whether he was Christian or Jew or Greek. Attention is concentrated on the power of Peter; and all else has passed out of memory. There is not the same detail or vividness here as in the account of the lame man at the gate of the Temple (III. 2 ff.). Luke's informant was so deeply penetrated with admiration for Peter that his narrative loses touch with the surroundings. But the incident produced a strong effect on the population of Sharon, the low ground between the mountains of Judea and the sea, at the eastern edge of which Lydda was situated; and thus it was remembered.

The other incident occurred at the sea-port of Joppa, the modern Jaffa, about ten miles north-west of Lydda. A widow called by the Aramaic name of Tabitha (i.e. Gazelle, in Greek Dorcas) had taken a leading part in the charities of the Church at Joppa; and it may be gathered from this case that there was an organization of charity at Lydda similar to that described already at Jerusalem, and that the work of voluntary helpers was carried on in a systematic way; though no record is preserved as to the official administration in those early churches of Palestine.

Tabitha died and was prepared for her grave: the body was washed and laid out ready for burial. It was known that Peter was not far distant, and messengers were sent to Lydda begging him to come. Now the ordinary Jewish custom was that the burial should take place very quickly after death. As a rule, at the present day, only a few hours elapse in those regions between death and burial: the washing and preparing of the corpse, the vehement mourning of the women, and the funeral, are performed with a celerity that is repugnant to our western minds. In this case it is not made clear why time was allowed to send and bring Peter. Possibly, he may have been asked to come when Tabitha was sick, in the hope that he might cure her as he had cured Aeneas; and he arrived only when she was laid out for burial. Possibly, the burial was delayed from the desire to do special honour to the deceased by having a great Church dignitary present (a desire which is at the present day always strong among the people of the Eastern Church), or in the vague hope that Peter might be able to do something and give some aid in the great calamity which had befallen the congregation at Joppa. The record is silent about these details. There is no hint as to the motives of the senders, the action of the messengers, the reasons stated to Peter, or the resolution that he formed to bring his abode and work in Lydda to an end. But the scene is put vividly before us when he reached Joppa, as he looked on the dead, and the widows stood by weeping and showing the clothes that Dorcas had made in her charitable work; and this scene perhaps tends to favour the last hypothesis stated about the reason for summoning Peter. In this incident, as in the cure of Aeneas, attention is concentrated on the power of Peter, and only what sets him in strong relief is remembered.

Faith is not mentioned by Luke as playing any part in this incident; but it may be understood that Peter here, as in III. 6, spoke "in the name of Jesus Christ of Nazareth," and that he would have said, as in III. 12, that it was not " by our own power or godliness" that this thing had happened, but that "by faith in His name hath His name" restored Tabitha to health. So also he said to Aeneas, "Jesus Christ healeth thee". On the other hand there could be no faith on the part of the dead Tabitha co-operating with the power of the Apostle, as there was in the case of the lame men in III. and in XIV. The narrator on whom Luke relied was wholly preoccupied with the thought of Peter's power; and this favours the opinion stated above, that he was one of those who had seen and been overwhelmingly impressed by the event. The description of the scene when Peter arrived at the house strongly suggests the account of an eye-witness before whose memory the visible details stood out clearly.

This narrative remains unique and unparalleled in the book, and yet it is the story told to Luke by one who saw and believed that Tabitha had died and lived again.

The incidental allusion to the widows of the town

showing the garments which Dorcas had made, brings us in contact with the facts of early Church life. Here we find the germ of the Order of Widows, which is mentioned by Paul in 1 Timothy v. 9 f., and which became very important in the following years. They devoted themselves to charity and good works in the congregation.

XIII

THE CAUSE AND MANNER OF THE GROWTH OF THE CHURCH

Review: Acts I.–IX.

IN the opening verses of the Acts the guiding idea of the book is clearly indicated. As the first book of Luke's history had shown the Divine Power made manifest among men in the man Jesus, "all that He began both to do and to teach," so the continuation of the history will show the continuous influence of the Divine Power, when no longer visible to the human senses, but only manifested in its effects.

The central idea throughout the book is the guidance of the Holy Spirit, which comes to reside in the hearts of such men as are fitted (i.e. are eagerly desirous) to receive it; the Spirit initiates and conducts to a successful issue all the action described in the book, moulds the Church, dictates the instructions which the Church issues to its converts (xv, 28), and makes the Church expand

78 XIII. THE GROWTH OF THE CHURCH

as a living organization over "all Judea and Samaria and unto the uttermost part of the earth".

Incidentally, we observe that the history does not reach its limits in the Acts. It has not at the present day reached its limits; but it continues "always even unto the end of the world". Whether the writing of Luke had reached the limit which he contemplated is a matter of doubt. Luke carries it down to the time when the new Faith was fixing itself firmly in Rome. Did Luke intend to stop there? The question has often been asked. The present writer would answer in the negative.

The growth of the Church through the influence of the Holy Spirit is one main topic and guiding interest of the author. This increasing strength is measured at first by numerical estimates, so long as numbers could be reckoned; 120 in I. 15, 3000 in II. 41, 5000 in IV. 4. Thereafter the complexity of the Church, and its extension over many synagogues and groups, prevented statements of that kind. No one could any longer survey the Church as a whole; numerical estimates were impossible; and the Apostles needed a supplementary body of Seven Officials to acquire the knowledge of individual needs which was required for the fair distribution of charity.

In the following stages the steps by which the

Church was spread over the world, are stated geographically. Samaria was included, then the maritime plain, and Galilee, Damascus, Phœnicia, Antioch, and on to the West. But those steps were not made by deliberate purpose and plan of the Church and its officials. The scattering of the Christians in the great persecution produced the first advance beyond Jerusalem and its neighbourhood. The Spirit ordered both the journey of Barnabas and Saul to the West, and the journey of Philip to the southern wilderness and afterwards to Ashdod and the cities near the sea. Only in the first action taken by Philip in Samaria does an official of the Church make an important advance which is not expressly attributed to the action of the Spirit, and in this exceptional case we see the effect of Philip's own modesty, which prevented him from claiming to have been honoured with a direct revelation of the Divine will.

The growth of organization in the Church was also a matter to which Luke devotes special attention. The first public act of the Church after the Ascension was to fill up the vacancy among the Apostles, and in the record of the proceedings the words bishopric, diaconate (twice), and apostleship are used as equivalent terms. Considering that the officials in the Philippian Church (with which Luke was closely connected) were bishops and deacons (Phil. I. 1), we must understand that it was a matter of interest to him to trace the development of these offices in the Western Churches for the purpose of taking the place of the apostolate in Jerusalem.

The historian describes with marked care the first step in the widening of the organization, viz. the appointment of the Seven, and shows how it arose out of the need and desire for efficient performance of the practical work of the Church. Good administration was necessary to make an efficient Church; the method adopted was a human device, not a Divine unchanging ordinance, for we never hear that this institution of the Seven was repeated elsewhere; but improved administration quickened the spiritual power of the Church. Two other classes of members of the Church at Jerusalem are mentioned, the young men (more accurately translated, the men of active age), v. 6, 10, and the elders, xv. 4: these seem not to be officials, but merely the result of a rough classification according to age and authority. Where the brethren are mentioned as doing any serious business, one may understand that the elder brethren were most prominent. Where active bodily work was in question, the younger would naturally come forward. Then in the congregation at Joppa we observe the germ of an Order of Widows, devoted to Church work, after their duties in their own families had ceased to engross their attention.

Being dependent on the oral tradition which he heard in Palestine, Luke in the early chapters has no exact statements of time (such as he often gives in his last chapters, where he writes as an eye-witness and contemporary), and he first alludes to contemporary events of general history in XI. 28 and XII. 20-23. But, by comparison with Paul's statements of years in Gal. I. 18, II. 1, we gather that the intervals between the events mentioned in the first eight chapters of the Acts were short. The conversion of Paul probably occurred early in A.D. 32,[1] rather less than three years after the Crucifixion. A certain interval had then elapsed since the death of Stephen, during which persecution raged in Jerusalem, and the Christian fugitives had time to settle in Damascus, and news about them to reach Jerusalem. Stephen's death fell probably in autumn 31, and the appointment of the Seven in late spring 31, before the harvest began, when the stock of corn was low, prices were high, and the poor felt the pinch of poverty, and those who thought themselves neglected were most likely to be complaining. The events described in Chapters

---

[1] We see no reason to doubt the tradition that it occurred on 25th January. The day was likely to be remembered in the Church.

I. to V. arrange themselves between spring 29 and 31. Philip's mission began in the winter of 31-32 and probably several years elapsed before he settled in Cæsarea. The progress of Peter "through all parts," evidently began after Paul's first visit to Jerusalem some time in 34; and he was in Jerusalem temporarily when Paul came there for the second time in 45, the fourteenth year after his conversion.

The date of Stephen's death is important. It shows how rapid was the development of the Church from the beginning. After the inspiration of Pentecost, we have a series of steps made at short intervals through the guidance of the indwelling Spirit to meet the external conditions. The Church was not inactive for a day after the coming of the Spirit at Pentecost. It was constantly exerting itself both in external growth through the preaching of the Word, and in internal development through the improvement of its administration and the organization of charity.

So Luke's history, when rightly understood, is fatal to that fashionable modern theory which regards the early Christians as simply waiting in expectation of the immediate coming of Jesus Christ to reign upon the earth. The confidence in the Kingdom of God which they felt was not a feeling that made them sit inactive; it roused them to strenuous activity and preparation. Every one was at work, each in his own way: Peter the leader, yet always ready to learn from the bolder initiative of others like Stephen and Philip. Each attempt to muzzle or suppress the new Faith only resulted in increasing the energy and widening the range of missionary effort.

XIV

THE UNIVERSAL GOSPEL

Acts x. 1-xi. 18

THE story of Cornelius is so crowded with interest that only a tithe of the points that rise in it can be touched upon; and it is better to speak more fully about a very few than to enumerate a larger proportion of the whole.

1. The importance of the episode in its bearing on the history of the young Church is shown by the space devoted to it. Luke always selects and groups his topics with great care and skill. Out of many things which he had seen and heard, he selects only a few; and he dwells upon these proportionately to the importance of each for his purpose as a historian. The story of Cornelius is not merely described at much greater length than any preceding incident. The important parts of the story are narrated twice, or oftener: Peter's vision (x. 11-16, xi. 5-10), Cornelius's vision (x. 3-6, 22,

30-32, xi. 13 f.), and several other details similarly. There is one striking parallel to this; the conversion of Paul is described three times in the book. The reiteration emphasizes the importance of each event.

2. The purpose of Peter's vision was not to intimate that God had abolished the distinction between food that was clean and permitted, and food that was unclean and forbidden. This distinction was founded on sound sanitary principles, suited to the climate. There is no reason to think that any intention is implied in x. 14 f. to permit or order Jews to eat creeping things. No one can well doubt that Peter continued as before to refrain from eating forbidden food. It may, however, reasonably be thought that the distinction was to be regarded henceforth, not as a mere ritualistic law, but as a rational principle based on sanitary considerations, and liable to vary in its details according to climate. Peter's own interpretation of the vision was stated by him to Cornelius and his friends, " Unto me hath God shewed that I should not call any man common or unclean ". The reference is here explicit; Peter understood that the vision was symbolic of human nature, and meant that all men were or could be cleansed by God.

Moreover, Peter recounted to the straitest

Jewish Christians in Jerusalem his vision and his consequent action; and they were all convinced and glorified God, not because He had abrogated the distinction of foods, but because "to the Gentiles also hath He granted repentance unto life".

This vision is a typical example of the symbolic or emblematic way of expressing spiritual truth, which is characteristic of Semitic and especially of Biblical expression. When Peter called the creeping things and quadrupeds and fowls "common and unclean," and was rebuked in the words, "what God hath cleansed, make not thou common," the person who insists on the literal interpretation about food misses the vast spiritual force, and also tramples on a sound principle of health in those southern lands. Christianity did not do away with what was healthy and good in Judaism, but completed what was defective and gave life to what was fossilized in it. The Jewish Christians saw the meaning of the vision at the moment in a vague way, though they did not comprehend all its broad significance. Paul had to work for years before the principle stated in this vision was fully recognized by the Church as a whole, though the leaders accepted it more quickly than the mass of the Jewish Christians.

3. The meaning of Peter's vision was de-

clared in the immediate result. He acted without hesitation on the invitation of a foreigner, a Roman officer, one of the army that held down the Jewish nation. He entered into his house and into familiar intercourse with him. He even ate with him. To hold conversation with an unclean foreigner, and even to enter into his house might be allowed to Jews; the six Jews of the circumcision who accompanied Peter did that. But Peter did more than Jewish custom permitted; and it is not stated that the six did as much; the general drift of Chapter XI. suggests that they did not eat with Cornelius, for the charge of having done so is made against Peter alone. The issue of the incident was the recognition by the Church that repentance, baptism, and the gift of the Holy Spirit were granted to the Gentiles also; but, though this was acknowledged to be the case with Cornelius, yet there was a widespread disinclination in Jerusalem to regard the principle as universal. Doubtless, it was pointed out by the Judaizing party in the Church at Jerusalem, that Cornelius was a person who had previously attached himself to the Jewish religion, for he " feared God with all his house, and gave much alms to the (Jewish) people and prayed to God alway," though he had never become fully a proselyte or complied with the whole Jewish Law. It seems therefore to have been still the prevalent view of the Jewish Christians in Jerusalem that foreigners should come into the Church in the same way as Cornelius; and apparently the expectation was entertained that, considering the close relation of Christianity to Judaism, the Gentile converts would accept the Jewish Law as binding on them, and live according to the double Law of Moses and of Christ (like the priests in VI. 7).

4. The vision of Cornelius is described in slightly varying terms: in X. 3 " he saw in a vision openly a messenger of God coming in unto him and saying"; in X. 22 "he was warned by a holy messenger"; in X. 30 "a man stood before me in bright apparel and said."; in XI. 13 "he had seen the messenger standing in his house". Here, as always, such slight divergences are mere matters of expression, varying attempts to put into inadequate human words the real Divine truth, which is above human language and beyond ordinary human thought.

5. Both visions are concerned with matters which must have been much in the minds of the two recipients at that time. On the one hand the relation of the new Church to the outer world must necessarily have been presenting itself to Peter. He could not have forgotten that the orders of Jesus were of universal application. The whole

world was to be the measure of the Church. Although in Jerusalem the problem was less pressing, yet as soon as Peter and Philip went out of the holy city, the question forced itself on them how they should treat the Gentiles, who were numerous in the sea-plain of Sharon, in Joppa, Ashdod, Lydda, and Cæsarea. The Divine Will here revealed itself to a man who was eager to find it, thinking of it, seeking after it, and praying for it. On the other hand, Cornelius was in a similar position. He was seeking to attain unto the light: his prayers were "gone up as a memorial before God". Philip was already in Cæsarea (VIII. 40); and in all probability Cornelius knew what he was declaring and perhaps had heard him. The vision of Cornelius was the answer to his prayer, and the solution of questions over which he had been pondering.

6. It is characteristic of Philip to be silent about his own share and to give all the credit to Peter. Similarly, at Samaria not a word is said about Philip's action after Peter appears on the scene. It is precisely the silence about Philip in this scene at Cæsarea, where Peter could hardly fail to come into relations with him during his stay, that shows his mind and his self-suppression. Philip, therefore, was Luke's authority for the Cæsarean incident. No other informant except

Philip would have left out Philip. It is equally evident that Philip was not his authority for the sequel at Jerusalem in Chapter XI. There is no reason to think that Philip went to Jerusalem with Peter.

XV

A MESSENGER OF THE LORD

Acts XII. 1-24

A PERSECUTION of a new kind is described in this chapter. Previously, persecution had been caused by Jewish dislike of innovation and of seeming disrespect to the Mosaic Law; but now the persecutor was the King Herod Agrippa I, who reigned from A.D. 41 to 44. No cause is stated for his action; but the narrative suggests that it originated in personal or dynastic motives, and was continued because Herod found that his first act, the execution of James, was popular among the Jews in Jerusalem, whose favour he was bent on gaining. The reason for his first act probably was that he regarded the preaching of the Kingdom of God as indicating disaffection towards his own kingship and danger to his dynasty.

The Pharisees and those who were zealous for the Jewish Law had been estranged from their previous friendliness to the new Faith by the outspoken preaching of Stephen; and they were glad to find a champion of their cause in the King, who now proceeded to imprison Peter. But, while the mass of the Jews were hostile, there is every reason to believe that in all ranks of Jewish society there were persons well disposed to the new Faith. Formerly, Jesus had devoted friends at the court of Herod Antipas, such as Joanna the wife of the King's steward, and Manaen the King's fosterbrother; and so now it is probable that there were in the court of Herod Agrippa friends ready to help Peter secretly, but not willing to sacrifice their career and openly profess the new Faith. In the following centuries of danger and suffering the Christians were often indebted to the kindness shown by persons of that class.

The situation in Jerusalem was critical. The Church was dismayed at the blow which threatened its leading spirit; and "prayer was made earnestly for him". Then follows the detailed and remarkable account of Peter's deliverance. Ultimately, he was himself the authority, as no other knew the facts and his own feelings and soliloquy, until he related them to a company of the Christians. From one or probably from several of those who listened on that night to Peter, as he told the story within a few minutes after his deliverance,

Luke heard what had occurred; and we may be confident that it is recorded precisely as Peter described it.

Peter was arrested during the days of Unleavened Bread, and his execution was postponed by the piety of Herod until the feast was ended; but he was guarded with the utmost care. Two soldiers were always in the cell with him, and his hands were fastened by two chains to his keepers,[1] while other two sentinels stood on guard outside the door. The duty of watching Peter was assigned to sixteen soldiers, four of whom took the duty in turn, three hours at a time. On the night following the last day of the feast, and on the eve of his execution, the prisoner was wakened from sleep by a blow on his side: "a messenger of the Lord stood by him, and a light shined in the cell". Of what nature the messenger of God was, whether a man (as in x. 3 compared with 30) or not, whether the guards were asleep, what were the exact circumstances of the release, we are left to conjecture, and it is evident that Peter did not explain to his hearers. The important matter was that a messenger of God had given effect to the Divine Will, and conducted the prisoner safely through all the guards to the outer gate (which

---

[1] His left hand was chained to one keeper, his right to the other.

opened to them of its own accord), and along one street, before leaving him.

Peter, who had been wakened suddenly out of a deep sleep, did not himself realize what was taking place. He thought that it was all a dream, and "wist not that it was true which was done by the angel" (i.e. messenger). The description of the situation and of his thoughts is marvellously graphic and lifelike. As we read it, we feel ourselves in the porch of Mary's house, listening to his eager, hurried narrative, and especially his reflections, when the angel left him, and he "was come to himself". Previously he had been only half awake and acting mechanically, but then he "knew of a truth that the Lord had sent forth His messenger, and delivered him out of the hand of Herod, and from all the expectation of the people of the Jews".

When Peter thought over his position, one street away from the prison and therefore still in imminent danger, he went to the house of Mary, a near relative of Barnabas and like him probably possessing some wealth, evidently a widow whose house was a customary meeting-place for the Christians. Peter was a friend of the family, and the slave-girl Rhoda, who answered his knock, instantly recognized his voice. The whole household and many others had assembled and were praying for Peter's safety at the very moment of his deliverance. The slave-girl shared the troubles and happiness of the family;[1] and now, excited with joy and losing all sense of her immediate duty, she left Peter outside in danger, while she ran in to relieve the anxiety of the household. Here another singularly vivid and charming picture is set before us; Peter knocking repeatedly outside; Rhoda delivering her glad news in fluttering joy; the people incredulous and calling her mad to say that Peter was there; Rhoda triumphing over their folly and persisting in her statement; the insistent knocking at the door; the amazement of all when they went out and beheld the escaped prisoner; Peter calming the excited throng with a motion of his hand, telling his story, sending a message to James (evidently now the recognized head of the Church), and going away to an unknown destination.

This incident was evidently described to Luke by an eye-witness. Only one who was present could have pictured it so vividly. We can understand that many who were in Mary's house that night would remember Peter's narrative, his words, feelings and thoughts, for all would regard him

[1] Domestic slaves were at that time treated generally as members of the family even in pagan, much more in Christian, households.

with the keenest interest. But who would remember the emotions and demeanour of the slave-girl except herself? Luke, however, had seen her, talked to her, heard her account of the scene, and with the skill of a literary artist perceived that it was more effective and revealed better the inmost character of the situation than the narrative of any other member of the Church whom he met in Jerusalem. Nowhere in the whole of this history is the authority whom Luke followed so clearly shown as here; and nowhere is there so beautiful a picture of life in the early Church, with its house-meetings and its familiar intercourse between all classes

To us in modern time the question appears of supreme moment whether this deliverance was accomplished by supernatural or by natural means. To the hearers on that night the question was of no importance, and does not seem to have suggested itself. To the Oriental mind the natural and the supernatural are one: any person who carried into effect the purpose of God to save His servant was His messenger. Is not the Oriental view the truer one? The trivial things that scholars often discuss and dispute about are not even mentioned by Peter; but the important things are there, the need of the Church, the earnest prayers of the people, and the help sent by God.

Is it wise or right for any of us to dispute who or what was the messenger of God on this occasion, and to declare that he who differs from our opinion is either on the one hand sceptical or on the other hand irrational? This narrative is a test case. It comes to us almost in Peter's own words, spoken within an hour after the event, and reported by a devoted mind that treasured every word. No better authority could be imagined except a letter of Peter describing the event; and this report is almost as good as a letter in respect of faithfulness, while it shows us the impression made at the time upon others better than even such a letter would. In it the natural and the supernatural meet on a higher plane of thought.

Peter did not reveal his destination to the household of Mary. Probably he wished them to be able to deny all knowledge where he had gone, in case his communication with them should be detected, and they should be arrested and questioned.

XVI

THE CONVERSION OF PAUL

Acts VIII. 1; IX. 1-22

SAUL OF TARSUS appears first in the scene of Stephen's death, as a man of active age (not necessarily a young man in our sense), taking a leading part in that terrible scene. He was already a person of influence in Jerusalem, marked out as a leader by his intense and devouring enthusiasm, especially where something exceptional or dangerous had to be done. The stoning of Stephen, though stoning was permitted by the Jewish Law in cases of exceptional and gross impiety, was dangerous to the perpetrators as being contrary to Roman law. This disgraceful act, and the even more disgraceful persecution which followed (more disgraceful because more cold-blooded and long-drawn-out), were performed under the superintendence of Saul. He made havoc of the Church for some time, during which occurred the first stage of Philip's mission in Samaria and the coast towns.

Under the Roman law the persecution must stop short of the death penalty. Though occasionally some exceptional act of Jewish religious frenzy, such as Stephen's murder, might be winked at, yet the Roman Government would not permit such acts to become habitual. Saul, therefore, having done all that was possible in Jerusalem, looked out for a new field of action.

Palestine offered none, for the Faith was only beginning to spread in the rest of the country. Moreover, the Roman rule curbed his action seriously, and prevented him from doing anything drastic, except where a large body of Jews, living together and amenable in religious matters to the Jewish Law, offered an opportunity.

He fixed his eyes, accordingly, on the great city of Damascus, which was outside the sphere of Roman law, and governed loosely by the barbarian King of Arabia. In such a city the close-knit fraternity of the Jews was permitted to exercise its own religious law very freely and fully. A large body of Jews had settled there and maintained their worship in several synagogues. Saul, either hearing or suspecting that the Faith had spread thither, sought and obtained letters from the high-priests and the Council or Sanhedrin (XXII 5) to the rulers of the synagogues in Damascus, commissioning him to seize all Christians and bring them to Jerusalem. It is evident that the rulers of the Jews in Jerusalem exercised authority in religious matters over the Jews abroad

We see here a proof that Sadducees (as the high-priests were) and Pharisees (who were influential in the Council) were united in hatred to the new Faith since Stephen had offended the latter. In Damascus, however, the Christians were still living at peace among their kinsmen as a school or sect of the Jews (IX. 10; XXII. 12), just as the Church in Jerusalem had done in the first two years after the Crucifixion.

Saul's journey to Damascus would naturally be made by the direct road, called "the Way of the Sea" (i.e. the Sea of Galilee), crossing the Jordan by the "bridge of Jacob's daughters" (as it is now called), a few miles above that sea. Modern travellers from Jerusalem to Damascus usually make a detour in order to see the sources of the Jordan and the Waters of Merom, and thence follow a different road to Jerusalem. The old tradition places the scene of the remarkable event that followed at Kaukab, where "the Way of the Sea" crosses a very slight ridge about twelve miles south of Damascus. Here the first view of Damascus burst on the persecutor's sight; "and suddenly there shone round about him a light out of heaven" "above the brightness of the sun," and the whole company fell to the ground. The others seem to have risen at once to their feet (IX. 7); and they comprehended little or nothing of what Saul describes as happening to him while he lay on the ground. Doubtless they went on to Damascus in due course, and mentioned as they sat at meat or over their wine a remarkable natural phenomenon that occurred by the way Jesus was not for them.

The scene is three times described in the Acts, twice by Saul in speeches to which Luke may perhaps have himself listened, and once by Luke in his narrative. The ultimate authority is in every case Saul; Luke tells what he had himself heard Saul narrate during their long and familiar intercourse. There are certain slight differences between the three descriptions. Luke must have been fully conscious of these variations, and, since he has allowed them to remain in his history, we must understand that Saul sometimes laid more emphasis on some points, sometimes on others; and that Luke was impressed by the variations and intentionally records them. In this we must not merely recognize the singular accuracy and honesty of the historian, but also we must infer that Luke regarded the differences as being characteristic of the scene. Saul was the best possible

XVI. THE CONVERSION OF PAUL

authority about what happened to himself; but he was so entirely absorbed in the vision that he was not aware exactly of what his companions did and felt.

In regard to the vision, attention may specially be directed to the following points :—

1. Saul both heard and saw the Lord. He lays most stress in his letter to the Corinthians on the fact that he had seen Him. He had no doubt as to this. He had seen, and he knew that Jesus, whom he had thought dead, was living and was Lord. This profound and unhesitating conviction that the same Jesus who had preached and been crucified was still living is most easily explained, if Saul had seen Him in His earthly life. Hence, like the Apostles, Saul was a witness that Jesus was not dead, but had risen.

2 The question is often asked whether the vision was objective or subjective, whether Saul saw or only imagined. It is recorded by Luke in the words of Saul that the other travellers saw no man. Saul alone saw Jesus. There is an element in the human being which must respond before communication can take place between the Divine power and the human nature. Saul alone could respond and see. But that the vision was real, Saul could never doubt. It was the most real event in his life. It changed his whole career. It

has altered the course of all history, and affected the entire world. The full comprehension of this great and marvellous event is fundamental in the Christian life. The more one ponders over it, and the better one understands it, the more real is one's grasp of the true nature of religion and of the true relation between God and man

3. There was no apparent preparation in Saul's recent life for his change of character. He was revelling in the full course of persecution. He was firmly persuaded that Jesus had been an impostor, and that for himself the one right work was to punish all who believed in Jesus, and to eradicate and destroy that belief. When he was at the height of his fanatical resolve, he was suddenly stopped and turned into another path by the heavenly vision.

4 Yet there was in Saul's past life a real preparation for his vision and his new career. In later meditation he recognized that his whole life had been a preparation, and that already before his birth the preparation had begun in the circumstances and situation of his family. He was born to be the Apostle of the Gentiles. He had been brought up from infancy in the Greek city of Tarsus as at once a citizen of that city and also a burgess of the imperial city Rome. He had been trained to a far wider outlook on the world than

XVI. THE CONVERSION OF PAUL

the people of Jerusalem could attain to. He knew the pagan world from inside, its needs, its desires, its religious longings, its weaknesses, and its crimes. He could appreciate the universality of the Saviour's life and message to the world in a more complete way than any of the Palestinian Christians. He had for the time been forced into alliance with the presecuting Jews of Jerusalem by the common hatred which he and they felt for the Jesus whom he misunderstood; but that alliance could not have been permanent. Saul was too wide and too bold in his views to remain a mere Pharisee. True comprehension of Jesus was needed to ripen Saul's character. This comprehension could not be attained until he had been disabused of the belief that Jesus was dead. The Lord revealed himself to him at the proper moment, and broke the barrier that was preventing the completion of Saul's education for the purpose of his life.

XVII

ORIGIN OF THE GREEK CHURCH

Acts XI. 19-30; XII. 25

THE new Churches, Samaria, Lydda, Joppa, even Cæsarea, were of secondary importance in the history of the Church, and are mentioned merely as steps in the growth of a young power. We come now to one of the great Churches of the Roman world.

Antioch of Syria was the first Gentile Church, and exercised, as such, a distinct influence at the time. The relation between Jews and Greeks in that great city raised the general question of Gentile rights in the Church, and after long controversy was settled by the first Council, a precursor of the Œcumenical Councils of later centuries.

Antioch afterwards became one of the five patriarchates of the Christian world; and her future dignity was foreshadowed in her importance at the first. It is remarkable that in general the history of the early Christian period is an anticipation, and so to say a prophetic forecast of the subsequent course of history; the same principles were at work, and there was a general similarity in their effect on the earlier and the later Roman Empire.

The Christians who were scattered at Stephen's death carried the Gospel wherever they went, and sowed broadcast the seed of the Church. In every city they found themselves at home among their own people and in their own synagogues; and they were still generally of the earliest Jewish-Christian type. They had not adopted the ideas of Stephen, but were still in the older stage when the Church seemed to be little more than a school or sect of Judaism with certain additional rules. Hence, wherever they went, they " spake only to the Jews "; Philip stood almost unique in his wider outlook. But the leaders of the Church endorsed Philip's action, and thus began a certain divergence of view between the leaders and the mass of the Jewish Church. In the Epistle to the Hebrews this divergence is implied as a very marked feature.

In Antioch a wider address was inaugurated by certain Christian Jews of Cyprus and Cyrene, who had been accustomed to live among Gentiles. They began to address themselves to those Greeks who had already been attracted by the simple and lofty religion of the Hebrews, and had thus come within the influence of the synagogues.

The religious position of these Antiochian Greeks was quite similar to that of Cornelius, but his case is described as a single one, whereas in Antioch many Greeks came over to the new Faith. The general principle was determined in the single case; but at Antioch a Church grew up composed mainly of Greeks, who, though friendly to the synagogue, had never been proselytes. Such was the origin of the first Greek or Gentile Church.

The new Faith now entered on its career in the Roman Empire, for so long as it was composed only of Jews and proselytes, it stood, in a sense, outside the Empire and in some degree outside of the Roman law, being amenable in all religious matters to the Jewish rules and the authority of the priests Now, even in religious matters, Christians of Greek birth were free from the Jewish authority and subject only to the law of the Empire. It was therefore in Antioch that the existence of the new sect as a part of the Empire was recognized; and then people devised a nickname by which they might speak about it; and thus in the slang of Antioch arose a term which became a title of honour afterwards, "Christians," the people of Christus.

As in the case of Philip's action in Samaria, the new step made at Antioch was sanctioned and accepted by the Church in Jerusalem, after an inspection had been made first by Barnabas and afterwards (as Paul mentions, Gal. II. 11) by Peter. Luke records only the former, and evidently regarded it as conclusive evidence of the Church's approval. Barnabas recognized the epoch-making character of the new step. He saw that the rapid growth of the Greek element in the Antiochian Church needed a man of peculiar qualifications. He perceived that Saul (whom he had met and appreciated in Jerusalem eight or nine years before) was the right man for the work, and he went to Tarsus and fetched him. This probably occurred in A.D. 43 or the early days of A.D. 44.

Immediately afterwards a step of supreme importance in consolidating the now scattered Churches was made. This step was of the kind which we saw to be important in the earliest Church at Jerusalem—it consisted in the organization of a Church fund for the relief of distress—but it was wider in character, for it applied money contributed in one city to relieve distress in another. This great step was made from a small and apparently accidental beginning. The prophet Agabus announced "that there should be great dearth over all the world"—not of course a universal failing of the crops in the same year in all parts—and this did in fact occur in many places during the reign of Claudius, A.D. 41-54. The Church in Antioch resolved to collect money and to send relief to the central and mother Church in Jerusalem. This plan formed the model for the contribution which Paul twelve years later arranged in the new Churches of Galatia, Asia, Macedonia, and Achaia, and which delegates carried to Jerusalem with them (Acts XX. 4, XXIV. 17, 1 Cor. XVI. 1-3).

Thus the principle was established that all parts and members of the Universal Church should help to support and stimulate the life of each other. The practical working out of this principle involved constant intercourse between the separate parts of the Church, the transmission of knowledge to all parts about everything that concerned every part, the interchange of ideas, the sending of letters, the travelling of individuals from congregation to congregation, the hospitable reception of every traveller wherever he went, the sense of unity and brotherhood brought home to every traveller by finding in all cities Christian friends believing and thinking like himself. This constant inter-communication was of inestimable importance; it was the circulation of the very life-blood of the Church.

The famine in Judea, as Josephus describes it,

was very severe, and the worst time was in 46 : these facts imply that the harvest failed in 44 and 45, and that the extreme of scarcity was reached just before the harvest of 46. The mission of Barnabas and Saul as the leaders of a deputation to carry help from Antioch occurred in A.D. 44.

The relation of Jews to Gentiles in the new Church was naturally a subject of discussion between the two envoys and the Apostles. The question whether the Greek converts should be required to conform to the Jewish Law was answered in the negative. These discussions seem to have occurred during private communications and conversations with the leading Apostles in Jerusalem; and no formal assembly of the Church was held. The time for public consultation had not yet come. The envoys were not empowered to lay the matter formally before the Church of Jerusalem; but they must already have perceived the questions and difficulties that must arise; and they were strengthened in their work at Antioch by the concurrence of the Apostles in all that they had done, and in their plans for the future relations between Jewish and Gentile Christians in the Antiochian congregation.

Saul seems to have hoped that this occasion, when he was bringing help to his people in their need, would afford a good opportunity of appealing to them and touching their hearts; but he was warned in a vision to depart from Jerusalem, "for I will send thee far hence unto the Gentiles". He was, however, now accepted by the leading Apostles, James and Cephas and John, as "entrusted with the Gospel of the pagans" in virtue of "the grace that was given unto" him, i.e. the vision and the direct commission of God.

The incidents of this visit to Jerusalem have to be pieced together from Acts XI. 29 f., XII. 25, and XXII. 17-21, and Galatians II. 1-10; and when placed side by side, the various details there mentioned suit each other perfectly.

XVIII

THE APPROACH TO THE GENTILES

Acts XIII. 1-12

As Luke described the government of the Church in Jerusalem by the Twelve, and the appointment of the Seven to co-operate with them when the volume of business increased, so at this point, after telling how the first Gentile Church was founded, and how it was united to the central body in Jerusalem by the tie of charity and service, he names the leaders of this new Church, Barnabas, Symeon Niger, Lucius a Cyrenaean, Menahem (in Greek Manaen), and Saul The order evidently gives the official precedence and dignity at this period, A.D. 45. Barnabas ranks first as representing the authority of the central Church, and as deputy of the Apostles, Saul last as the youngest and latest. The other three are evidently the early founders of the Antiochian Church. The order is that of the moment. Shortly afterwards no one would have thought of placing Saul last.

The five ranked as "prophets and teachers". They were marked out by their individual gifts as leaders; and the administration of the Antiochian Church was analogous to that of Jerusalem.

There were not, as yet, in the Gentile Church any officers bearing an official title, such as bishop or deacon. There were only men of eminent spiritual power, who on that account administered the work of the Church. The careful precision with which Luke marks the character of Church government in this early time shows that he appreciated thoroughly the importance of orderly administration, and that it was his intention to indicate the steps by which administrative methods were elaborated. About sixteen years later Paul wrote to the congregation in Philippi with its bishops and deacons; in the interval the government of Gentile Churches had been more definitely organized. About sixteen years earlier Peter, only a few days after the Resurrection, had spoken of "bishopric" and "deaconship" as the sphere of duty of the Apostles. The old Greek religious term "liturgy" is chosen by Luke to describe the sphere of duty of the five prophets and teachers in Antioch.

In the course of their ministration and fasting, the message of God was made known to them that the hour had arrived for beginning the special work

XVIII. THE APPROACH TO THE GENTILES

to which Barnabas and Saul had been called. A previous call is here mentioned. The summons which had been given to Saul has already been described;[1] but we do not learn how or when it came to Barnabas. We know only that the two returned together from Jerusalem to Antioch, and at the proper moment (probably in the spring of A.D. 46) they were ordered to begin their work.

It is not stated that their work was defined. Apparently its exact character and sphere was not known. It had to be discovered by doing it; and when the two missionaries returned to Antioch it was recognized by the Church that they had fulfilled it (XIV. 26). We also must discover what it was by reading the account of their work.

The Church of Antioch sent them forth, releasing them from their duties there. The Church of Antioch received them again on their return (XIV. 27). It was thereby marked out as the Mother-Church of the Pauline congregations; and it ranks henceforth as more truly the directing and moving power in the Universal Church than Jerusalem was.

The Church of Antioch sent them forth; but also the Holy Spirit sent them forth. The action of the assembled congregation is the action of the Spirit, alike at Antioch (XIII. 4) and at Jerusalem (XV. 28).

[1] See Section XVII.

The two Apostles went down to Seleucia, the harbour of Antioch, and sailed for Cyprus, where they made a missionary progress through the island, beginning from Salamis. Nothing that called for permanent record occurred, until they reached Paphos, the capital city at the western end of the island, where the Roman governor lived. This lack of record does not imply want of information on Luke's part, but only that the procedure in Cyprus was exactly similar to what had occurred in Syria and Palestine: the Apostles everywhere addressed the congregations in the synagogues, including doubtless the "God-fearing" Gentiles [1] who had been attracted to attend, but they did not directly [2] appeal to the Gentiles. No new step was made, until at Paphos the Proconsul, Sergius Paulus, invited Barnabas and Saul to explain their doctrine to him. This Roman official was "a man of understanding," interested in philosophic and scientific studies, and he desired to hear what these new teachers of philosophy had to say.

[1] The numerous Gentiles, who had been attracted by the lofty and austere doctrines of Judaism, and who formed a sort of outer circle round the synagogues, are commonly called by Luke "God-fearing" or "devout" (as in Acts XVII. 17, but not "devout" as in VIII. 2 different words in the Greek).

[2] "Directly" means amid the surrounding of Gentile life, and not in the assemblies of the Jews.

At this point the Apostles came in contact with a Jew named Bar-Jesus, one of those magicians, similar to Simon of Samaria, who were so common in the ancient Greek and Roman world. Such persons were, generally, of the same character, possessing a certain stock of real knowledge about the powers and processes of nature, which they eked out in varying degrees by imposture and fraudulent tricks. To judge from the brief account given by Luke, Bar-Jesus seems to have been rather more of an impostor and less of a believer in his own aims and powers than Simon; but still he had sufficient knowledge to impose on a man of understanding like Sergius Paulus and to be received among his personal friends.

The magician forthwith recognized that the newly arrived Jews were dangerous rivals. He doubtless regarded them as persons of his own class, bent on obtaining reputation, influence and fortune by public exhibition of their knowledge and their powers; and he sought to turn away the Proconsul from listening to them. Thus the scene was turned into a direct combat between the one power and the other, between the sorcerer or false prophet Bar-Jesus and the preachers of the true Faith.

There, in a hall or an open court of the Proconsul's palace, the contest was fought. We are left to imagine the earlier stages. The narrative moves on to the point where the magician, observing the effect which the words of Barnabas and Saul were exerting on the Roman, and dreading that they might supplant him in the favour of the great man, tried to interrupt the hearing. Perhaps he sought to cast ridicule on the speakers. Certainly he attempted to misrepresent and distort the history of Jesus, whom they were preaching, and thus " pervert the right ways of the Lord ". Perhaps he tried to impress the Proconsul by some tricky exhibition of his power. In one way or another he roused the enthusiasm and wrath of Saul, who, though hitherto secondary to Barnabas, now assumed the foremost place. We can imagine him making a step forward, transported with the indwelling power of the Holy Spirit, and fixing his blazing eyes on the sorcerer, who cowered and shrivelled beneath that terrible gaze and the terrible words that accompanied it. Some such withering effect is clearly implied in the act that followed. Bar-Jesus lost all power of resistance and all will-power; he was helpless before the denunciation of the Apostle. As he heard the voice of doom that he should be blind for a time, he tottered about in the hall, groping for some one who might guide him.

This marvellous scene is the first in which the

XVIII. THE APPROACH TO THE GENTILES

Gospel was presented direct to a Gentile (and doubtless to a group of Gentiles, the attendants on the Proconsul), wholly unprepared by previous participation in the teaching of the synagogues. Without intending it, and without seeking the opportunity, the Apostles had "turned to the Gentiles"; and the occasion was consecrated and marked as epoch-making by a wonderful exhibition of spiritual power.

In this moment, filled with the Spirit, Saul steps into the position of leader; and at the same moment his Jewish name Saul drops from him in the historian's mind and narrative. His Greek and Roman name Paulus is now mentioned for the first time, and henceforth he stands before us in Luke's pages as the Roman or Greek Paul. He moves henceforth in the Greek and Roman world as a member of it, bearing a name that belongs to it. It happened that the Greek and Roman name of the Apostle was the same as the last name of the Proconsul; but this was a mere accident. Saul had possessed from childhood the name Paulus. He was born in a double rank, a Jew among Jews, and a Roman Tarsian among Romans and Hellenes; and he had two names corresponding to his double rank. Among Jews he was named Saul; and hitherto we have seen him in that character. Among Greeks and Romans his name was Paulus, and henceforth we shall see him in this character. The transition from the one stage to the other is indicated by the use of the alternative names, "Saul otherwise called Paul".

Further, we must observe that Barnabas is henceforth mentioned by Luke only in the second place, with rare exceptions, as at Jerusalem, where the old rank and order were observed in the Apostolic decree (xv. 12, 25). Saul the Jew was second to Barnabas the Jew; but Paul was first wherever he went On Paul all eyes were concentrated, alike of friends and of enemies. But now and henceforth he is not simply the Hebrew and the Pharisee, he is the citizen and the Evangelist of the Gentile world.

XIX

PAUL TURNS TO THE GENTILES

Acts XIII. 13-52

THE dramatic scene at Paphos did not lead to any further development at the moment; and the Apostles went on to Perga, the chief city of Pamphylia. The sea-road from Syria to Rome led along these coasts. Already Christians had gone to Rome, and the new Faith was known in the capital of the world. Probably some idea of working along the coasts of the Roman voyage may have been in the mind of Paul already, and may have guided his steps gradually westwards.

However that may be, a complete change of scene was resolved upon at Perga. No reason is stated; but that some change of plan occurred seems proved by the fact that Mark now abandoned the work and returned home. The others crossed the great extent of mountains that lay to the north of Perga, a difficult and even dangerous journey of more than a hundred miles, and came to Pisidian Antioch, an important city, a Roman

Colony,[1] the military and administrative centre of the southern half of the vast Province called Galatia by the Romans.

Here they were received with a hearty welcome, which deeply touched Paul's heart. Afterwards, when writing to all the Galatian Churches, he recalls the warmth of their kindness to him and their ready reception of his message; and he lays stress on the fact that they welcomed him thus, although he came afflicted in a way that was a severe test of their hospitality and kindness. This affliction was a disease, "an infirmity of the flesh," which was considered in those lands as a proof of Divine wrath and curse, and usually caused the sufferer to be despised and treated as an outcast. Paul, however, was regarded by the people of the Province Galatia as "a messenger of God" (Gal. IV. 13).

This illness which afflicted Paul is elsewhere described by him as a serious hindrance to his work, striking him down suddenly and often. He mentions also that this disease was the reason why he came to preach the Gospel in the cities of Galatia. His words show plainly that he had a serious illness in Perga, and on that account the scene of work was changed from the enervating

[1] Colony, i.e. garrison city, in which Roman settlers and soldiers with their families constituted a privileged aristocracy.

XIX. PAUL TURNS TO THE GENTILES

coast lands to the high plateau where the Galatian cities lay. At the moment the defection of Mark was keenly felt by the sufferer; and for years he retained a distrust of Mark, though in the end they became again fellow-workers.

The narrative in the Acts illustrates and confirms in a striking way the picture given in Paul's letters. The Apostles came to Antioch, and on the first Sabbath they were invited by the rulers of the synagogue to address the congregation. The brief narrative is silent as to the reasons for this invitation; and we can only guess at them. But such is Luke's method: he states the facts, but is usually silent as to the circumstances which in his view were unimportant. What was important in the historian's view was the address delivered by Paul, who had now become the leader and the chief speaker.

This was, apparently, the first time that Paul had preached since the Paphian scene. His views were now broadened; and here, for the first time, Luke gives us a report of a sermon by Paul. He recognized that now at last Paul had perceived his true vocation, and this is selected as a typical discourse. It therefore deserves careful study.

The first thing that we observe is that Paul addresses himself not to the Jews alone, but to Jews and the God-fearing Gentiles equally. It is evident that there was a number of the latter class present in the synagogue, persons previously inclined towards the simple and lofty religion of Judaism; and that they attracted the notice even of a stranger. In his opening words Paul appealed to the two classes of hearers separately; and in verse 17 the word "our" refers to the Jews alone. In verse 26, the two classes of hearers are again mentioned and are both called "brethren," and summed up together "to us is the word of this salvation sent forth". Here for the first time is the Pauline Gospel declared; we are all equal, all brethren, all alike in the new Faith. In verse 38, the entire congregation is appealed to as "brethren" simply; the distinction of the two classes has been forgotten; there is only one class in the Gospel, there is remission of sins for all; all who believe are justified. To this Paul adds that the Law of Moses was not able to save them from their sins.

The effect of this address was extraordinary. Luke speaks as emphatically on this point as Paul in Galatians IV. 13 f. On the next Sabbath, about ten days after the Apostles had arrived,[1] "almost the whole city was gathered together to hear the word". The message of Paul was accepted by

[1] As regards this matter of time, the writer took a wrong view in "St. Paul the Traveller and the Roman Citizen," p. 99 f The error is corrected in the "Cities of St. Paul," p. 298.

the Gentiles as their own. The Jews on the contrary felt a grudge. They began to realize more than they had at first all that was implied in Paul's Gospel.

In Pisidian Antioch general good feeling had evidently reigned between the Jews and their fellow-citizens. The former were comparatively open-minded and free from bigotry. They were quite willing to welcome the Gentiles as hearers in the synagogue, and to extend religious patronage to them. But they were not willing to regard them as equals and brothers. Now, like Bar-Jesus at Paphos, they "contradicted the things which were spoken by Paul, and blasphemed". Thereupon Paul pronounced the final words of severance, "we turn to the Gentiles". To the Gentiles he addressed himself henceforth primarily in Antioch. The whole region of which Antioch was the central city was gradually affected by the preaching of Paul. This would take place through the various causes which brought to that great Roman Colony and centre of government the inhabitants of the smaller towns. Paul and Barnabas seem to have resided continuously in Antioch, and trusted to these public gatherings to reach the wider audience of the region.

The Jews were not idle. They possessed great influence with the ladies of the higher class in

Antioch, i.e. the wives of the Roman colonists, and with their husbands the chief men of the Colony. Luke does not state the steps by which the Jews effected their end. There must have been some accusation, a trial, and a sentence. In all probability one of the three cases in which Paul was beaten by the rods of lictors, occurred as the result of this trial and as the preliminary to expulsion, for it was only in Roman colonies that this kind of action could occur. In Antioch the colonial magistrates were attended by lictors.

Thus the Apostles were finally expelled from the city. How long they had resided in it cannot be gathered with certainty from the narrative; but, though the city was very quickly affected by the new Faith, some lapse of time must have occurred while the whole region around Antioch was being permeated; and it is necessary to reckon the stay there as extending over several months. It may be thought that the Jews would have succeeded sooner in expelling them; but it has to be remembered that Roman law ruled in the Colony, and that some sufficiently plausible cause had to be found before peaceable strangers could be punished and expelled.

If we assume, as seems probable, that this missionary journey began in the spring of the year, several months must have been spent in evangelizing all the cities of Cyprus and in going to Perga. Mt. Taurus could not well be crossed by the travellers later than October, and probably the journey from Perga took place as early as August or September. The ancient custom was to avoid travelling in the winter season. The winter of A.D. 46-47 was spent in Antioch.

XX

THE CHURCHES OF GALATIA

Acts XIV. 1-30

AFTER their expulsion from Antioch the two Apostles came to Iconium. But the new Church, which they were leaving behind, was already strong enough to be self-supporting. It was not young and delicate, and in need of the daily help and guidance of its founders. It was " filled with joy and with the Holy Spirit," entering with good hope and brave heart on the new life. This description confirms the picture given by Paul himself in his letter to the Galatians of the extraordinary vigour and the fervid spirit which characterized the Galatian Churches from the beginning.

If we compare this state of things with the anxiety that Paul on his next journey felt about Thessalonica, when he had to leave it too early, we feel that his residence in Antioch must have been long enough to educate the people of the city and the region round about it in the principles and practice of the Faith; and we must conclude that the whole winter of A.D. 46-47 was spent in the city. Moreover, the ancients were as a rule inclined to regard travelling in the winter on the plateau as impossible. Just as soldiers did not march or fight in winter, so people did not travel in that season, as appears, for example, from Basil's letters, written in the fourth century; though modern American missionaries in Turkey make light of the hardships involved in winter travel. Antioch is about 3500 feet above sea-level; a considerable tract of high mountains separates it from Iconium, which is 3370 feet above the sea; and the climate in this region during winter is very severe.

In Iconium also the Apostles had great success. They began, as usual, with teaching in the synagogue; and "a great multitude both of Jews and of Greeks believed". Here again, as in Antioch, it seems to be implied that there existed a friendly relation between the Jews and the Gentiles of the city; so that the preaching in the synagogue came immediately before many Gentiles, who had already been under the influence of the pure and lofty morality of the Old Testament. Thus a considerable Church was built up rapidly in Iconium.

Mischief again arose from the disbelieving Jews, who, by ways that are not described, set the unconverted part of the Gentile population at enmity with the Apostles. Yet the latter remained there in spite of the growing opposition, and taught boldly in public for a long time. This long period must include most of the spring and summer of A.D. 47.

The difference of opinion in the city grew stronger; and it is well known that among the ancients public feeling resented such differences as hostile to the unity which ought to exist in a city, and regarded the persons who had caused such differences as enemies of the public peace, without enquiring whether their acts were justifiable or not. It was sufficient that their presence and conduct had caused dissension in the city.

Thus the unbelieving Jews had their hands strengthened against the Apostles. The end was brought about by mob violence, and not by formal action of the magistrates as at Antioch. Paul and Barnabas learned that there was a plot "to entreat them shamefully and to stone them". Such expressions point to illegal and riotous conspiracy.

The Apostles yielded to the storm, and fled to the adjoining country of Lycaonia, viz. that part of Lycaonia which was in the Roman Province Galatia, and which contained two cities, Lystra and Derbe, along with a large number of villages. Iconium was reckoned by popular native opinion as a city of the region Phrygia, and in their flight the Apostles crossed a frontier marked by change of nationality and of language; from the old Phrygian city Iconium they fled to the Lycaonian cities Lystra and Derbe; but all these cities alike were included by the Romans in the Province which they called Galatia.

Lystra, barely eighteen miles from Iconium, was the city where the Apostles first settled. It was, like Antioch, a Roman Colony, so that its population contained a sprinkling of Romans (who formed a sort of local aristocracy) and some Hellenes, together with a large number of the old Lycaonian natives. There were also some Jews, though Luke does not speak of a synagogue.

The history mentions in a general way that at Iconium "signs and wonders" were wrought by the hands of the Apostles, and these words are confirmed by the allusion which Paul makes in writing to the Galatians (III. 5); but at Lystra Luke describes in careful detail the healing of a lame man, which was followed by a great popular demonstration. The multitude (by which term the historian seems to mean the non-Roman part of the population in this Roman colonial city) expressed in their native Lycaonian tongue the belief that their visitors were not mere men, but gods come down from heaven in human form; and they made preparations to offer sacrifice to their

Divine visitants. In front of Lystra, which was situated on a hill in the middle of a level fertile river valley, was the temple of Jupiter, and the priest brought oxen decked with garlands to the portals of this temple. Barnabas, who was the more stately and dignified of the two, was regarded by the populace as Jupiter, while Paul, who was the chief speaker, was worshipped as Mercury, the messenger and herald of the chief god.[1] With difficulty the Apostles restrained the ardour of their votaries, explaining that their own aim was to turn away the Gentiles from such vain ceremonies to the worship of the true God, who, after leaving mankind in past generations to walk in their own ways, had now sent His Apostles to proclaim His true nature to the world.

Soon, however, the changeable mob was swayed to the opposite side by Jews from Antioch and Iconium, who excited a riot against Paul, as the more active of the pair, and after stoning him dragged his body out of the city. We notice here that the stoning took place inside the city. It was a riotous act; and the Jews who took part in it had no scruple in profaning a pagan city by such an act. In the murder of Stephen, on the contrary,

[1] An inscription recently found near Lystra groups together the same two deities.

which was done in strict accordance with Jewish procedure, though it was in Roman law an act of riot, the sufferer was taken outside of the city before he was stoned. It also deserves notice how carefully Luke refrains from going beyond the evidence. He does not say that Paul was dead, but only that the mob supposed him to be dead. Paul, however, was able to rise up and return into Lystra; and on the morrow he went with Barnabas to Derbe.

Nothing is recorded about the work in Derbe, except a general statement as to its success. From thence the Apostles, instead of returning by the short and direct road through the Cilician Gates and Tarsus to Syrian Antioch, resolved to retrace their steps in order to review and confirm the Churches which they had founded. From Lystra and Iconium they had been driven by mob violence, and they had legal right to go back at any time; but from Antioch they had been expelled by authority of the magistrates, and it may be thought strange that they could return to that city. The expulsion, however, did not carry any permanent disability; the magistrates had authority to expel persons who seemed to be a cause of disorder; but this was only a temporary measure, and the exiles could return at a later time on the chance that they might be permitted to remain; and it rested with the magistrates of the year to take cognizance of them or to ignore them, as they chose.

The chief act of the Apostles on their return journey was to provide for the organization and government of the new Galatian Churches, and now we hear for the first time of the election of presbyters by the congregation. The Greek verb must imply this method of appointment, though Paul and Barnabas are the subject of the sentence. The officials are called presbyters, i.e. elders. In Jerusalem it would appear that the presbyters were simply the older and more experienced members of the congregation. In Galatia, they were formally appointed officials, charged with the duties of teaching and administration, and apparently performing in these new Churches similar duties to those which were performed in Jerusalem by the Twelve and the Seven. From Galatia Paul and Barnabas crossed Taurus (probably in A.D. 48, certainly in the summer season) and returned through Pamphylia to Syrian Antioch, having completed the duty with which they had been charged.

Thus Antioch became the Mother-Church of all Gentile Churches.

XXI

THE UNION OF JEWS AND GENTILES IN THE CHURCH

Acts xv. 1-35; *Gal.* ii. 11 ff.

NOT less than two and a half years can safely be allowed for the epoch-making journey of Paul and Barnabas, considering the numerous cities where they preached, the extent of ground that they covered, and the length of time that they stayed in Iconium, and comparing the analogy of later journeys. They returned to Syrian Antioch, at the earliest, in the autumn of A.D. 48.

The situation in the Church was materially altered by this journey: when the two Apostles "turned to the Gentiles," the Church must likewise do so. The enthusiastic reception of the Faith by the Galatians could not be rejected or denied. We may regard it as almost certain that already the larger part of the Christian Church was Gentile. So long as merely single Gentiles here and there, like Cornelius, had come into the

Faith, the Jewish Christians might hope that such converts would conform to the Jewish Law, which was almost universally observed in the Church, or they might shut their eyes to some isolated exceptions like Titus. Thus the Church would still remain an essentially national institution, the perfected form of Judaism, into which the Gentiles were one by one admitted. The Church in Syrian Antioch had begun to show that the case was not so simple; and some private harmonious conversation had taken place on the subject in A.D. 45 between Paul and the Church leaders in Jerusalem (as is mentioned in Gal. II. 10[1]). But only the leaders had at that time seen the deeper issues that were involved. The Christian public in Jerusalem did not as yet look below the surface. Now the facts were forced on their notice by rumour from the north, while Paul and Barnabas "tarried no little time with the disciples" in Antioch, i.e. in the year 49.

It was apparently at this time that Peter, in his progress round all the Churches, came to Antioch (Gal. II. 11). In accordance with the understanding already formed between the leaders and Paul, he did in Antioch as he had done in the house of Cornelius: he lived familiarly with the Gentile Christians, and ate with them. But certain men

[1] See Section XVII.

that came down from Judea ("from James," i.e. officially sent from the head of the Judean Church, as is stated in Gal. II. 12) were shocked at this way of life; and they stated plainly the view which had lain deep in the ordinary Jewish mind throughout these proceedings. If the Gentiles were to enter the Church, they must comply with the Jewish Law; they could not be received straight from paganism into the full communion of the Church; there was too deep a chasm of thought and life and morality separating Jews and pagans; "except they be circumcised after the custom of Moses, they cannot be saved". Now Paul also recognized the chasm that divided pagans from Jews; he fully admitted that the pagans must rise to the higher moral level of the Jewish religion, if they were to enter the Church; but he maintained that a mere external ceremony like circumcision was immaterial, and that it was the moral character of the Mosaic Law which the Gentiles must put on before they could be saved. Peter, however, was so far influenced by the Jews that he withdrew from familiar intercourse with the Gentile Christians in Antioch, admitting practically that Jews and Gentiles could not meet at the table of the Lord, unless the latter accepted the Jewish rite. Paul rebuked Peter for this defection, and the issue is not stated. But the dissension grew sharper in Antioch, and at last it was resolved to lay the whole matter before the Apostles and the Church in Jerusalem.

This was an important step. Antioch admitted that the unity of the Church implied the recognition of Jerusalem as the authoritative centre of the whole body. As before it had sent help in time of famine, A.D. 44, so now it sent delegates, Paul and Barnabas and certain others, to seek advice. The delegates were escorted on their way by the Church of Antioch, whose sympathies were entirely with them; and as they traversed Phœnicia and Samaria, "they declared the conversion of the Gentiles," causing great joy. It was quite evident that a vastly wider movement than the formation of a Judaistic Church was imminent, and that issues of world-wide character depended on the decision in Jerusalem.

When the Church met to welcome the delegates, they described the wondrous success in Galatia and the expectation of the Gentiles; but the Pharisees who had accepted the Faith urged that all these Gentile converts must conform to the whole Mosaic Law; and the meeting was adjourned for further consideration. The second meeting was long, and much discussion took place, in which the Antiochian delegates and their opponents stated the arguments on their respective sides. Luke describes this debate in two words, and hastens on to the point where Peter intervened to relate his own experience, that God had decided the case by giving the Holy Spirit equally to Gentiles and to Jews. His speech produced a hush in the assembly; and Barnabas and Paul reinforced his argument from the facts by "rehearsing what signs and wonders God had wrought among the Gentiles by them".

After such testimony it was recognized as impossible to insist that the Mosaic ceremonial was necessary, when the Spirit and power had been granted to multitudes who were ceremonially unclean. God had shown that the mere ritual of the Law was not a necessary requirement. James, who evidently presided as the recognized head of the Church, summed up the manifest feeling of the meeting by a conclusive speech, welcoming the Gentiles to the Faith, setting aside for them many of the ceremonial requirements of the Law, but insisting on its moral demand, the prohibition of all impurity in life. He also required, as a concession to Jewish feeling and as almost necessary to render free intercourse possible between Christian Jews and Gentiles, that the Gentiles should abstain from eating the meat of animals that had been sacrificed to idols or any meat which had not been fully freed from blood.

Without these conditions it was impossible for social communion to exist between Jews and Gentiles, for all Jews were bound to refrain from such meat, and if Gentile Christians placed it on the table and partook of it, Jewish Christians would be unable to sit with them. If these conditions were observed James, strict Jew as he was, saw no reason why Christians of all nations should not meet at the common meal; and his view was published as the Decree of the Holy Spirit and of the entire Church.

It seems, at first sight, strange to us that one moral condition of the most fundamental and necessary kind should be placed among the ceremonial conditions, which in our view are of comparatively minor importance. But moral purity of life was so systematically and universally disregarded in even the best circles of paganism, that the Christian teachers were compelled to emphasize its overwhelming importance, not merely by urging it along with the other moral duties of life, but also by publishing it as one of the conditions of Christian social intercourse. We may illustrate the position from modern social life: not merely do we teach temperance as one of the moral duties, but also we make it a social principle that any person who is guilty of intemperance is excluded from society; and the social law is more effective

XXI. THE UNION OF JEWS AND GENTILES

with many persons than considerations of moral duty.

The Decree of the Council was an attempt to combine the Jews and the Gentiles permanently in one Church. It was accepted by the leaders. It was acquiesced in at the moment by the rest of the Jewish Christians, but without hearty goodwill. A division grew up between them and the Gentile Christians. The greatest Jews, such as Peter and John, turned their attention more and more to the latter. The divergence of feeling in Jerusalem led to the writing a few years later of the Epistle to the Hebrews, which attempted to persuade the reluctant Jewish Christians.[1] The difference of sentiment, however, was too strong. The Jewish section of the Church gradually died out after a century. There was then nothing to gain by observing the ceremonial prohibitions of the Council, and only the moral side of the Decree was enforced finally by the Church.

[1] We date this Epistle in spring A.D. 59, shortly before Festus arrived (Acts XXV. i.); and we understand that it was written with Paul's approval and after much conversation with him, by the head of the Church in Cæsareia, viz. Philip.

XXII

FAITH AND WORKS

James II. 14-26

THE Epistle of James is inspired by the desire to resist and extirpate certain faults that became manifest in the Church as it grew stronger and acquired a large body of adherents. The two opening chapters are directed largely against a dangerous misapprehension of one of the fundamental principles on which Paul insisted most strongly. Christianity is the religion of an educated and thoughtful people; and only those who rise to the full comprehension of its doctrine, and who steadily live more and more intensely, and grow morally stronger as they grow older, can maintain themselves on the true level of the Faith. The great Pauline doctrine of justification by faith was one which the unthinking multitude would easily misunderstand and misapply. James has to deal with this misapplication

His letter therefore belongs in point of date to a

stage in development following immediately upon the preaching of Paul. When James declares that " by works a man is justified, and not only by faith," he is not contradicting Paul's statement that " a man is not justified by the works of the Law save through faith in Jesus Christ " : he is correcting a false view as to the meaning of Paul's words. When he asks " was not our father Abraham—was not Rahab—justified by works ? " he is expressing an apparent, but not a real, dissent from Paul and from the writer of the Epistle to the Hebrews, who quoted Abraham and Rahab as examples of faith. James sees and says emphatically about Abraham " that faith wrought with his works, and by works was faith made perfect ". He saw that faith and works must go hand-in-hand, and he protests against the separation which some had made between them.

He emphasized the truth that "faith without works is dead ". But he also, in the opening words of his letter, lays the strongest emphasis on the power of faith. " If any of you lacketh wisdom, let him ask of God, and it shall be given him : but let him ask in faith, doubting nothing " He who doubts must not " think that he shall receive anything of the Lord ".

These passages show that faith was to James, as much as to Paul, a fundamental requirement in religion. To the man who prays without perfect faith God grants nothing. To him who prays with faith God grants even wisdom, the greatest, the highest, the most difficult gift in human nature to bestow. He to whom wisdom is granted has all things granted to him. It is the poor men who are "rich in faith and heirs of the kingdom" (II. 5). Having faith they have salvation. James, therefore, acknowledges emphatically the supreme power of faith; but it is not his purpose to insist on this. Others had done so sufficiently, and James's slight allusions imply the prevalence and strength of the doctrine in the Church.

But it was easy to talk of faith, and to mean by it something essentially different from what Paul had in mind. To Paul faith implied a change and remaking of the whole nature, so that the man who believed must inevitably carry his faith into action. Faith in the Pauline sense could not exist without producing what James calls works. Faith was to Paul a power, and not a mere quality or characteristic. Faith drove the man on to act. Faith possessed and ruled the man. "It is no longer I that live, but Christ that liveth in me:" every man who had true faith, and was justified by faith, could say for himself those words of Paul: Christ lived and worked in him. But it was quite possible to apply the words "faith" and "belief" to a certain purely intellectual appreciation of the truth, or an appreciation so weak in moral quality that it could not remake the man's nature. Paul would have refused to acknowledge such a quality as deserving the great name of "faith". James saw that people who thought themselves, and were thought by others to be, members of the Christian Church, were making the great mistake and regarding such empty intellectual belief as "faith"; and he perceived that it was not sufficient to tell them that this quality was not really "faith". It was necessary to be far more emphatic, to denounce the error, and to bring its nature home to the minds of his hearers and readers. It was not, as they thought, sufficient for salvation to believe that Jesus was the Christ. Nor was it, among the vulgar, sufficient even to declare that true belief would work itself out in life and action. Stronger emphasis was needed to penetrate deaf ears and dull or prejudiced minds.

Hence the vigorous and thorough-going way in which James denounces the error. He points out that belief alone may be perfectly right, and yet perfectly inefficacious. The devils also believe and tremble; they recognize the nature and divinity and power of Jesus, and tremble before Him; but they are no nearer salvation on that account. The only safe rule, therefore, for the ordinary man is to insist that faith without works cannot give salvation. Such faith is not the living and transforming power that Paul preached: it is dead. Look at the life and the acts and works of every man, and do not estimate him on his words and professions. If you see a fellow-Christian in rags or starving, and content yourself with words of consolation and sympathy, such as "go in peace; may you be warmed and fed," and do not give him what is needed for his physical comfort, what is the good of your faith and your sympathetic kindly words? Any one, whether learned and clever or plain and simple, can see the truth of this. Every one whom you meet will in practice make the same criticism, and will say, "You have faith, and I have works: I can by my works demonstrate to you my faith; but can you show me your faith apart from your works: I want some proof of it? I need something that I can see and appreciate, before I take your faith as real: I cannot take it on credit merely because you talk finely about it." Such is the plain fact of life. Such is the rough practical sense of the ordinary man. Faith apart from works is barren; it produces no good for the Church, for the neighbours, or for the man himself.

Then James appeals to examples which would be familiar to all Christians. Abraham was the great type of faith; he believed in the Promise of God, when all appearance and probability was against its fulfilment. But Abraham's faith showed itself in act. He offered up Isaac his son upon the altar, when God seemed to ask it. His faith was made perfect in the actions of his life, and hence his belief was reckoned unto him for righteousness; but the faith alone without the works in which it practically manifested itself would not have justified him. So also Rahab, who served as another favourite illustration of the power of faith, was justified not only by faith but by the work in which her faith made itself effective and real.

James and Paul then are in reality perfectly harmonious; but James warns the generation which had listened to Paul against a misinterpretation of his teaching.

XXIII

WORD AND ACT

James III. 1-12

THE introduction of the custom of electing the Church officials by the votes of the congregation was almost inevitable in the Hellenic Churches. The habit of self-government by free popular voting was deeply engrained in the Greek nature, and the Church followed the national bent.

This seems to have been a new departure introduced in the Galatian cities. In Palestine the selection of a twelfth Apostle to fill the place of Judas had been left to the Divine choice between two persons who were put forward by a procedure which is not specified; and so also the exact method whereby the Seven were selected is not described by Luke. But in neither case is there even the slightest probability that voting was the method employed; and in the second case the Greek word which is used makes that quite certain. Doubtless in both cases discussion showed that certain individuals had commended themselves by their past life to the judgment of the best and most trusted members of the community. Opinions were weighed, and not counted.

In the Hellenic cities the Greek method of voting was apparently put in practice, as the Greek term (Acts XIV. 23) probably shows, though the English translation hides the nature of the process. The free voting stimulated public interest, and without it the spark of life could not easily have been kept effective in a congregation of Hellenes. The free Hellenic education and custom tended this way, counting all men equal.

Serious dangers, however, were involved in this kind of action. The method implied candidature; and with candidature came rivalry; and out of rivalry sprang jealousy, quarrels, factions, and divisions. The rival candidates had their supporters and partisans; and elections of Church officials became disfigured by strife. Paul alludes to these evils, and warns both the Galatians and the Corinthians against them.

James was also aware of this feature of Church life; but the aspect of it which most offended him was the eagerness of the members of the congregations in the West to speak and teach in public. All were eager to teach: few were ready to listen and to be taught. All were eager to recommend themselves to the public. Too many had an eye to future office, and were preparing for their candidature hereafter by keeping themselves well before the eyes of the congregation. That is the fault most characteristic of the Greek character throughout history; as a race they are fluent, talkative, fond of ostentation, and generally devoid of reticence and deficient in dignity; and that side of their nature was specially offensive to the graver mind of a Jew like James.

Hence the burden of his advice to his readers is that they be swift to hear and slow to speak (I. 19); and he now devotes a weighty paragraph to warn them against their besetting fault. They should not be eager for the official position of a teacher, and they should not be desirous to show off their powers as teachers unofficially. If the teacher has more influence and receives more respect and even pay, more is expected of him and he is judged more severely. We all make mistakes, we all stumble, both teachers and pupils; but the teacher is more harshly criticized, while the hearers are not condemned so readily.

The only duty of the Church officials which James alludes to is that of teaching. The Epistle belongs to a very early period, when Church doctrine and service were very simple, and when the duty of teaching, both in the conversion of the pagans and in the instruction of the converts, completely outweighed the other functions of the officials in the congregation. On the other hand the letter is later than the formation of the Pauline Churches, and has in view the faults that were characteristic of those congregations, and not the faults to which the older Palestinian Churches were most prone. We can, then, hardly doubt that James was addressing the new Churches of the West. When he calls them "the twelve Tribes which are of the Dispersion," he is speaking from the point of view which might be expected, and which is peculiarly characteristic of his school and his period. He had joined with Peter and with John in approving the action and mission of Paul. He welcomed the Gentiles into the Church. He was ready to accept them on the same level as the Jews in the Christian unity. But he still regarded the Gentile Christians as persons who were received into the Jewish pale. The Church was the kingdom of God; but it was a Jewish kingdom, which drew all nations unto it, and the Gentiles became "the twelve Tribes which are in the world outside of Palestine".

By an easy transition James passes from the general idea of stumbling to the particular form in which stumbling is most common and easy. "If any man stumbleth not in word, the same is a

perfect man, able to bridle the whole body also."
The hasty, idle, and foolish word was the most
difficult thing for these Greek Christians to avoid,
and it was the beginning of many dangerous evils.
It is a small and slight thing in itself, but it may
determine the direction of the whole life, as the
bridle and bit in the horse's mouth, or the small
rudder in the great ship, determines the whole
course of each. The tongue of a man, small as
it is, utters great and swelling words, and drives
him on to important issues in action, which he had
not thought of when he began to talk. It is like a
fire which spreads through the whole course and
order of nature ; but the fire is originally kindled
from hell, and the hasty word is suggested by the
devil. The tongue is the one thing in the whole
world that has never been tamed , birds and beasts,
reptiles and fishes, have all been tamed by man,
and employed for his use or his pleasure ; " but the
tongue can no man tame ".

Its unreasonableness, too, and its double nature,
are shown by the fact that it utters both blessings
and curses. This ought not to be so ; it is utterly
unnatural, and there is nothing similar to it in the
whole universe. Everything else is and does and
produces after its kind. The fountain gives either
sweet water or bitter, but never both. The fig-tree
produces only figs, and men never gather olives

from a vine. But the tongue is the one unnatural, incomprehensible, double-natured thing. We cannot tell what it will say: we cannot predict, as a man is opening his mouth, whether good words or bad, whether wise words or foolish, will come forth from it. Still less can we forecast what crime and misery may issue from the foolish and thoughtless word which the tongue utters.

XXIV

THE NATURE AND POWER OF FAITH

Hebrews XI. 1-30

THE Epistle to the Hebrews was written, as we think, in early summer, A.D. 59, towards the conclusion of Paul's imprisonment in Cæsarea. It was composed by some person who was in close relation and frequent communication with the prisoner; and its intention was to recommend the latter's views to the mass of the Jewish Christians in Jerusalem, who were suspicious of him and inclined to dislike his bold Gentile teaching. The author does not directly explain or defend Paul. He expounds the religious situation, and leads his readers to a point of view from which they might understand Paul better.

The leaders in Jerusalem were in sympathy with Paul, as he and Luke both tell us; and this Epistle distinguishes between the leaders and the mass of the Church, and addresses itself to the latter. The writer was in full accord with Paul, but expresses his own opinions after his own fashion, which is markedly different from the Pauline fashion. In this chapter, by words and examples which would be most easily intelligible to his Jewish readers, he explains the way in which he understands Paul's fundamental doctrine of justification by faith.

What the Christian hopes for, what is promised to him, is not given to him at the present moment, and is not anything that he can see or hold in his hands; but through faith he feels assured and firmly convinced that his hope will be given to him in due season. The men of older time are recorded in the Scriptures as patterns to all Christians, because they had faith and through faith believed that the Promise would be fulfilled to Israel, though they never saw its fulfilment. We, by faith, believe that God created the material world out of an immaterial origin, though we can never actually see or know how the creative act was performed.

Some of the examples of faith, which are selected from old Hebrew history, seem to depend on the Jewish tradition, which told more than is recorded in the Scriptures. We do not easily understand from Genesis how Abel and Enoch are examples of faith: the references to them in that book are too slight. In some way that is not recorded Abel's sacrifice was a proof of his faith, and was on that account accepted. Similarly, the translation of Enoch proved his faith; and the writer feels in this case that he must explain. Enoch had believed that God really is, and that God rewards those who seek after Him. Now paganism and idolatry in all forms are inconsistent with faith, because they contain a false idea of God. The pagan does not know what is the nature of God; he either is afraid of his God, and seeks to propitiate the anger of the deity, and prevent the Divine power from doing him harm, or he tries to make a bargain, promising certain gifts in return, if his God helps him. Such were the ideas of pagan worship; and they are inconsistent with faith. But Enoch had risen above the ideas of paganism, and attained to a true conception of the nature and kindness of God, and his faith in God had its reward.

Noah, when all others disbelieved, had faith that that which was told him would happen; and he prepared the ark to save himself and his household from an unseen and future danger. His faith in the coming punishment of crime condemned those who would not believe that crime should be punished.

Abraham, when he was bidden to go away into a strange land and leave his own people, had faith that good would result from his obedience, and that the Promise would be fulfilled in a distant future. Hence he became a wanderer in a strange land, a mere nomad, yet he had faith that a divinely built city would be given to his descendants. He firmly believed that his posterity would be numerous as the sand and the stars, although he and his wife Sarah were childless until extreme old age; and then, when his only son was still young, he was ready to sacrifice him at the command of God. Isaac and Jacob, on their deathbeds, blessed their sons, and with the confidence of faith promised them future happiness, as yet unrealized. Joseph showed faith in the future deliverance of Israel from Egypt, and ordered that his bones should be carried out when his people were sent forth. The whole history of Moses shows the triumph of faith. At every stage his parents and himself and the people whom he led took great risks, and preferred the future to the present, trusting to the words of a Promise in spite of the dangers and difficulties involved in this belief. So even Rahab, an alien, a Gentile, a pagan and a sinner, was saved by her firm confidence that the true God was fighting against her people.

These heroes of old all died without seeing their faith justified and their hopes realized (verses 13-16). Christ was not to come in their time; but by their faith they anticipated His coming, and He became a real possession to them. They said plainly that they were mere travellers and strangers in the world, and this proved that they regarded a heavenly country as their own, and that they lived in the confident hope of coming at last into their own land and their true home.

In this way one might go through the whole of Hebrew history, quoting from every page examples of faith. Every deed of heroism was done through the strength which faith gives. Every case in which persecution was nobly endured was a triumph of faith. Gideon, Barak, Samson, Jephthah, David, Samuel, the great prophets of Israel— all furnish examples of faith. The victories of the Hebrews in war were gained by faith, often against overwhelming numbers. In the book of Daniel we hear that the prophet was unharmed by the lions, and the three Hebrew children by the fire. Their faith saved them. To mothers who had faith their dead sons were given back. The sufferings and tortures which heroes and heroines of Israel endured were numberless and terrible. They were killed by the most painful lingering tortures. They were fugitives, skulking in caves, or wandering in deserts. It was through faith that they endured.

Yet all of these glorious models and patterns believed in that which was unseen and unknown. They never in life received the Promise. The

XXIV. THE NATURE AND POWER OF FAITH

completion and perfection of their hope lay among us, who have known the Coming of the Christ. They had to wait until our time for the realization of their faith. We are the happy ones, in whose time this realization has taken place. Surely, when we contemplate the history of our own Hebrew race, and observe so many witnesses testifying by their life to the power of faith, we cannot but be convinced, and live the life of truth, and follow the example of Jesus in perfect confidence. We must have faith in what is still unseen and future. We have to believe in the Kingdom of Heaven and in the second Coming of Jesus. We must have faith also in what is past and can no longer be seen, the life and the death of Jesus on our behalf. By belief in these, they become real for us, and they make part of our life and nature.

The whole argument proceeds from a Jew to Jews. The author pleads with his own brethren and identifies himself with their case. His object is not such a trivial one as merely to prove that Paul was right. Paul himself had no desire for that. He is preaching the Gospel of Paul from his own point of view and in his own way, eager to make his brothers in Israel feel themselves truly his brothers in Christ.

XXV

CHRISTIANITY GIVING VITALITY TO THE ANCIENT CIVILIZATION

Review : Acts x.-xv.

IN Section XIII a review was given of the growth of the primitive Church in Jerusalem, and of its diffusion over the Jewish and semi-Jewish population in the towns of Palestine. We have seen that for a short time it appeared to the human eye as if the young Church was to settle down into a mere sect—strict and advanced in tone, but still a mere sect—of Judaism. This was due to the natural, but too narrow, idea that the kingdom of God was to have Jerusalem as its centre, and that the whole world was to conform to the Jewish Law, and thus enter into fellowship with Christ. Stephen shattered this idea, and the Church as a whole accepted his views. The persecution that broke out after his death scattered the first Christians—known afterwards as "the ancient disciples" (Acts xxi. 16) —and caused a wide dissemination of the new Faith.

XXV. CHRISTIANITY AND ANCIENT CIVILIZATION

The doctrine of Stephen, in all that it implied, was not at first fully understood even by the leaders like Peter. Philip, one of the Seven, took the first step in widening the religious circle. Then Peter was warned in a vision that he should not call any man common or unclean, but that in every nation he that feareth God and worketh righteousness is acceptable to Him. After some dissension and discussion the Church in Jerusalem approved of Peter's action in admitting the Roman Cornelius as a member of the Universal Church, even though he had not conformed fully to the Jewish Law. By this action of the Church Peter's conduct in eating with Cornelius was tacitly condoned, though subsequent events showed that it was not really approved by the mass of the Jewish Christians, who acquiesced outwardly in the action of their leaders, but inwardly were far from being reconciled to the free admission of Gentiles into the Church.

The whole question was opened up in an acute form after the foundation of the first Gentile Church at Antioch. Luke does not expressly say whether the Gentile members complied with the Jewish Law; but he apparently assumes that his readers were aware that neither Cornelius nor the Antiochian Greek Christians did so; and Paul, in writing to the Galatians, asserts this about Titus. The whole history of the period shows that the Jewish

Law was not accepted in its entirety as binding in the Antiochian Church. But, although the Greeks of Antioch continued to be ceremonially unclean, it was not until a later stage that the question whether a Jew could lawfully associate with them was formally raised; and the circumstances prove that the earlier Jewish leaders in Antioch mixed freely with the Greeks. It may be presumed that the difficulty about meat was solved by them in the same way as was afterwards approved in the Apostolic Council.

Before the question was raised, another step had been made. The new Gentile Church in its turn began to send forth missionaries on its own authority, and thus to assert its recognition of the duty imposed on all Christians to educate, to Christianize, and to civilize the world. The journey of Paul and Barnabas was commissioned directly and solely from Antioch, so far as it had any earthly origin. Paul himself always asserted that he had no commission or charge from the older Church of Jerusalem and its leaders. The action of the Antiochian Church in sending out the two missionaries was ordered by the Holy Spirit; and this Church might say with as much justice as the Church of Jerusalem in the Decree of the Apostolic Council: "it seemed good to the Holy Spirit and to us".

XXV. CHRISTIANITY AND ANCIENT CIVILIZATION

The absolute independence and equality before Heaven of the new Church in Antioch was thus clearly and emphatically expressed. In this there was a danger, which might easily have become real and serious, but which was averted by the wisdom and faith of the Antiochian leaders. This danger was that, in the assertion of its independence, Antioch might separate itself from Jerusalem, and thus break up the unity of the infant Church. Any pride or arrogance or too strong self-assertion in Antioch, any emphatic resolve to assert its own rights, would have caused this result. The manner in which it was avoided is instructive as an example of the combination of practical sense, lively sympathy with distress, and readiness to hear the Divine voice and obey it. To all who believe in the Divine guidance and eagerly desire to follow it, the Divine voice will make itself audible. Charity to the poor, strong sense of brotherhood amid diversity, and recognition of the just claim of their distant brethren to be consulted on great questions, so that there should be a uniform spirit and tone in their policy, dictated the action of the Antiochian Church, and cemented the unity of the Universal Church.

The two most important steps, as recorded by Luke, in this epoch-making period, on which the whole future history of the Christian Faith and the sense of brotherhood in the entire Church depended, were the unasked sending of help to Jerusalem in view of the coming famine, and the consultation of the Apostles and Elders in Jerusalem about the relation between Jews and Gentiles in the Church. The meaning and importance of each of those steps has already been described. Here we have only to make four remarks :—

1. Luke does not attribute this wise action of the Church leaders to any preconceived plan. He makes it clear at every stage that the leaders were not working out any carefully formed scheme of their own. Each step was taken under the coercion of external circumstances. Sometimes a previously unimportant and little-known person made the new step. Sometimes persons standing wholly outside the Church, by persecution or otherwise, caused a new departure of great historical significance.

2. The leaders were always ready to learn from each new situation and from any person, and to take up an idea new to them.

3. The real moving power throughout was the Holy Spirit. The profound belief in its guidance was the one principle, according to Luke, which the leaders had in mind. To follow this guidance was, to them and to their historian, true statesmanship. They saw one idea always before them, the Death

and the Resurrection of Jesus; and this triumph of life over death was their message to the pagan world.

4. It is impossible to express too strongly the deep significance of the change which took place between A.D. 32 and 48. The attitude of the Church was turned in the opposite direction. Instead of seeking to bring the Gentiles into conformity with Judaism, it had now to face a totally different problem; was it possible to retain the Jews within its bounds? The Gentiles, the teeming population of the Roman Empire, were pouring into the Church, and threatening to drown out Judaism. Their overwhelming numbers were irresistible. Their eagerness was the most marked feature of the situation. Paul was deeply impressed in Galatia with this ardour of the Gentiles; and though perhaps the eagerness was hardly so great elsewhere, yet in every province of the Empire and in every city it was very strong. The civilized world was eager for the peace and the promise of the new Faith. The fields were ripe for the harvest. The fullness of time was come; and at that moment the Divine power made itself manifest. The Christian religion came in to cement the unity of the Roman Empire, to preserve the ancient civilization and law in its best features for modern men, and to strengthen the Empire for

the struggle against destruction by the barbarians. In the never-ending war between civilization and barbarism, between light and darkness, it had for a time seemed that the victory must be with the powers of evil, for civilization itself had grown weak with corruption; but the new Faith gave life and sweetness to the decay of the ancient world.

The Resurrection of Jesus was the saving element in the ancient pagan world. But in this change what was to become of the little people of the Jews? They held aloof, except the leaders, and as time passed they became more and more aloof; they shrank into their own retirement, and refused to be merged in the great world. The attempt made at the Apostolic Council to effect a *modus vivendi* between the two elements in the Church was unsuccessful in reconciling the mass of the Jewish Christians to their Gentile brethren.

XXVI

THE MOTIVE POWER OF LIFE

Romans XIII. 1-14

WE have seen how James explained in simple words and through examples drawn from past history, his view of the nature and practical effect of faith. Paul in writing to the Romans states in the language of the deepest and most philosophic religious thought his own conception of faith. James emphasized the plain practical fact that the faith which does not work itself out in the life and conduct of a man is dead. Paul, while apparently exalting faith and depreciating works, was thinking of the works that are done because a formal law commands them. He conceived faith as an intense and burning enthusiasm inspired through overpowering belief in and realization of the nature of Jesus—an enthusiasm which drives on the man in whose soul it reigns to live the life of Jesus. This overmastering faith makes the man's life, and shows itself in every act that he does. But his works are not done through an external command, because the Law bids him do them. They are the way in which his soul expresses itself. They are his life: it is no longer he himself, as a human being distinguishable from his faith, that lives. The faith that is in him is the one thing that lives and acts.

From a different point of view this faith which possesses the man and lives in him may be described as love. Faith in Jesus is an intense and supreme love for God, for all that God has made, and for all that is like God. The one supreme duty, the one thing that we owe to all other men, i.e. what we owe our neighbour, is love. It is easy to pay to our neighbour all the ordinary debts of life, all the debts that law recognizes and enforces; but there is one thing which is always due from us to all men, one thing which we can never pay completely, one debt that always remains still to be satisfied, and that is the love which we are bound to feel and show towards them.

This duty sums up and comprises in itself the entire law of conduct towards other men. He that has in his soul the true faith, or in other words the real love, has fulfilled the whole law, and much more than the whole law. The law, being a positive and external command, or series of commands, cannot do more than state a number of details—" thou shalt not steal," " thou shalt not commit murder," and so on. But no such enumeration of details can ever be complete; it must always fall short of the vast fullness and complicated relations of life. One may in a sense fulfil all those positive enactments, one by one, and yet fall hopelessly short of real goodness. Moreover, in the multitude of details, the man who is striving merely to obey the law that orders each action becomes befogged, and wanders from the true path. The details often seem to conflict with one another; questions of casuistry arise, and the law is not a clear enough guide. No one can be justified merely by doing the works of the law. The one true guide is the spirit of love and faith burning in his heart, impelling him to act, and showing him in each case what to do and how to do it.

There is another strong motive which should impel mankind to an active and strenuous life. The Day of Judgment and the Coming of the Lord are at hand. Every man should live in expectation. That day is nearer than it was. Each day spent is a day nearer the end. Life is not a time for sluggishness and sleep. In the darkness of night, sleep is permissible; but the night is now near an end, and the light of day is about to begin.

Paul's words when he refers to this subject are always mystic and obscure—not that there is really any obscurity in them, but that he has to express in human thought, which is conditioned by time, the idea of eternity which stands above and outside of and apart from time. That which is real and eternal must necessarily stand very close to us. Human nature is temporary, evanescent and unreal; it is here for a moment or an hour, and then it passes away; and yet it has a hold upon and a share in what is fixed and eternal. But the eternal does not come after the temporary; it does not begin when that which is evanescent ends; it is the real truth present in and underlying the changeable and unreal. Because it is real and eternal it is close at hand; it is here and now. But inasmuch as man's nature is imperfect, and because even the good man who is justified is still only straining after the truth, and struggling to reach what is beyond him, therefore the eternal and the real is apart from him, distant and hidden in the future.

Hence arises the apparent contradiction between Paul's language at different times with regard to the Coming of the Lord. Sometimes he emphasizes its nearness, when he desires to impress on people that it is certain and inevitable, and that every man must face it and ought to live in view of it. At other times, he has to remind them that many things must happen before the Lord comes, that the history of the world must continue and reach another stage in the development of the will and purpose of God as a preliminary. In the present chapter Paul's object is to make the great and final issue an incentive to immediate activity. That is what we have to live for, and we must live for it here and now, not begin to do so at some future time.

He employs here another kind of metaphor (which is one of his favourite forms of expression): the actions of a man's life are the dress which he wears. In the dark night, when one is free to live idle and to sleep, one wears the loose and easy garments that are suited for sleeping. But in the day one must put on other garments suited for active life in the open. With this is worked in yet another metaphor. The life of the Christian is a continuous warfare against evil and wrong. The true Christian is a soldier, and he must wear the garb of a soldier, the offensive and defensive armour with which all soldiers in that age, Roman or Greek or barbarian, were equipped. We must recognize, therefore, that day is now beginning, and we must put on the armour that becomes us to wear in the light of day.

Then in simpler words, and in another metaphor, Paul describes life as a walk. Since we are going about in the full light of day, there must be no pretence and no sham: "let us walk honestly as in the day ". Even the pagans of the world reserve their worst faults of personal conduct for the evening and the night. The revel at nightfall is accompanied by drinking, and leads on to vicious indulgence. Nothing of this can fill any part of the Christian's life. In the day the life of the pagan is guided by jealousy against his neighbour and competition with his rival. This also is unfit for the Christian and must be abandoned by him. His life is a warfare, but the war is not against his neighbour, as is the case with the pagan; the strife in which he is engaged is against the powers of evil and of darkness. He is to put on Christ as the armour of his battle, and to identify himself with his Leader. The war which he fights is the war of Christ against the world, and he is to give his whole mind to this, and to take no thought for his own bodily comfort and pleasures

XXVII

THE ENTRANCE OF THE GOSPEL INTO EUROPE

Acts xv. 36–xvi 15

THE mission of Paul and Barnabas to the Council in Jerusalem was followed by a short period of teaching and preaching in Antioch, which apparently comprised only a few months at the beginning of A.D. 50. It was probably in the spring of that year that Paul proposed to Barnabas to return to Galatia and "visit the brethren in every city" where they had preached. The spring is almost certainly the season when they would enter upon their journey, just as they would start in the morning, not in the afternoon. Such was and is Oriental custom and nature. The start probably was made in quite early spring, as the plan was to do some work by the way in Syria and Cilicia; and the beginning of summer is the season best suited for the long journeys which they proposed to make beyond the snowy Taurus and in Galatia, where the cities were placed about 3300 to 3600 feet above sea-level.

An unhappy incident now occurred, which led to the separation of Paul and Barnabas. The latter wished to take his relative, John Mark, as their companion. Paul, who had been deeply wounded by Mark's desertion on the former journey, would not trust him again. There was a sharp contention between the two old friends; and Barnabas went off with Mark to Cyprus, while Paul chose Silas, a delegate sent by the Council from Jerusalem The expression of xv. 37 seems designed to show that the Antiochian Church sympathized rather with Paul, who was continuing the forward movement, than with Barnabas, who went away into the backwater of Cyprus and passes out of history. Luke expresses no opinion as to who was to blame for the lamentable quarrel, and we should admire and imitate his reticence. The fate of the Church lay in the work of Paul and his coadjutors. We part from the honourable and gracious personality of Barnabas with deep regret; but history marches with Paul.

Some time was spent by Paul among the Churches of North Syria and Cilicia. These Churches are mentioned explicitly only here; and they are implied in xv. 23, where the letter of the

Council is addressed to them as well as to Antioch. Of their foundation no record is preserved. Presumably, they grew up partly through the work of Paul in A.D. 35-43 (Gal. I. 23), aided by the natural spread of the new Faith first in the towns along the great road connecting Antioch with Tarsus, and afterwards in outlying places. The facts of the situation show that they were mixed congregations, where the relation of Jew and Gentile Christians would be a difficult problem. Accordingly, the letter of the Council, fixing the terms on which social intercourse could take place freely between the converted pagans, who had been used to a looser life, and the Jewish Christians, who had grown up in the teaching of a stricter ritual and a higher morality, was addressed to all the Churches of the great united Roman Province, Syria and Cilicia; and there was no need for Paul to communicate the letter to them. His work here was only to "confirm the Churches," spending probably some days in each, enforcing the principles which they had already been taught

Thereafter, a long journey of at least 120 miles had to be made through a country which was not Roman, and in which Paul seems not to have preached, as it did not offer a favourable opening. His work began anew when he reached the Roman Province Galatia, and came first to Derbe, the frontier city, and then to Lystra. Here and in the other Galatian Churches the Decree of the Council had not yet been delivered, as it was not addressed to them. But the problem with which the Decree dealt was as acute in Galatia as in Syria and Cilicia. Paul loyally carried out the spirit of the Council's decision, communicating the Decree to his converts and urging them to keep it. His object was to secure unity of feeling and unity of life in those mixed congregations, where the former pagans were the overwhelming majority. No real unity was possible, if either the Jewish Christians insisted that the pagan converts should accept the whole Jewish Law, or the pagans refrained from complying with those enactments which were necessary if Jews were to sit at the same table and eat the same food with them.

Paul, in his eager desire to show the utmost respect to the Jewish Law in any case of doubt, took now a step which led to much discussion. He found that a youth named Timotheos (Timothy) at Lystra was a suitable coadjutor. A convert of Paul's former journey, he had acquired a high reputation in the congregations of his own country, Lystra and Iconium: Derbe, which was more distant from Lystra, is not mentioned. He was also marked out by prophetic utterances

XXVII. THE GOSPEL IN EUROPE

(1 Tim. I. 18); probably in the public assembly at Lystra some persons had suddenly, under Divine inspiration, designated Timothy for this work.

There was, however, one difficulty. Timothy was son of a Greek father and a Jewish mother. While his mother had trained him from childhood in the Jewish Scriptures, he ranked according to his father as a Greek, and had not been circumcised. It was almost impossible for him in this condition to come into social and friendly relations with Jews. His mother's marriage, it is true, proves that some Jews in that region were very free in their views, but the stricter Jews would be suspicious of the son of a mixed marriage, and would refuse to have any relations with him, unless he were circumcised. Yet Paul's method always was to begin with the Synagogue in each city, and a coadjutor whom the Jews would not admit to intimacy would be much less useful. Accordingly, "because of the Jews that were in those parts," he himself circumcised Timothy.

This action was easily liable to misunderstanding, as if it implied that ordinary Christians might be free from the Law, but that those who were to be worthy of higher dignity must comply fully with its requirements. Also, it shows that Paul entertained much wider plans than were stated at the start (xv. 36); his action to Timothy was intended, not with a view to the people of the already existing congregations, who thought so highly of the young man, but for the Jews of strange cities. Evidently, he was already planning his entrance into the great and wealthy cities of the province Asia.

But after surveying all his Churches, and seeing that they were steadily growing under the officials who had been appointed, he found at the frontier of Galatia and Asia that the Holy Spirit forbade him to speak the word in the latter province. The little company of travellers, therefore, turned north with the design of entering Bithynia, a rich province containing great cities; but "when they were come over against Mysia," their farther way northwards was stopped by "the Spirit of Jesus". They then turned westwards till they reached Troas. This journey, after leaving Galatia, was entirely in the province Asia, where they were not allowed to preach; hence they "passed by" (i.e. neglected) Mysia.[1]

The noteworthy difference of expression regarding the several intimations of the Divine Will points to different methods of revelation, and is obscure to us; but it springs from intimate knowledge on

[1] Mysia was a region of the province Asia · to reach Troas they must pass through Mysia, but did not preach in it

the part of Luke, and this knowledge was gained from Paul's mouth. We gather only that the second intimation merely barred the path to Bithynia, while the first gave clear orders as to conduct, but left the way through Asia open.

Now at last the explanation of these long journeyings came through a vision. By night Paul saw a man, whom he recognized as Macedonian, beseeching him and saying, "Come over into Macedonia and help us". Here Luke appears personally as one of Paul's companions: "straightway we sought to go forth into Macedonia, supposing that God had called us to preach the Gospel unto them". From this point onwards we can see where Luke left and rejoined Paul, by noting the use of the first personal plural pronoun. The intention is unmistakable. Luke desires to show clearly that in certain parts of the narrative he spoke as an eye-witness. If so, it must also be inferred that in the rest of the book he was not an eye-witness, but depended on the authority of others. In XIV. 22 "we" is used differently; it means "we Christians" universally; but in XVI.-XXVIII. it marks the writer as one of a small company of travellers, who are all called to be preachers and missionaries. It was at Troas that Luke began to be a companion of Paul; he remained in Philippi when Paul went on; later, when Paul returned to Philippi, Luke rejoined him and accompanied him to Jerusalem and Rome. These and other facts point to some connexion between Luke and Philippi.

Philippi, a Roman Colony and a leading city of its district, was reached by a voyage to Neapolis and a short journey inland. It contained few Jews and no Synagogue. When some days had passed, and the Sabbath came, Paul's party went out to the river-side, and found an assembly of women met for prayer. This offered an opening, and they addressed the women. One of these was a stranger from Thyatira, whose national appellation Lydia had supplanted her proper name. Although not a Jewess, she had been attracted by the severe and lofty Jewish religion. She was now deeply impressed by the new teaching, and after a time, evidently short, she and all her household adopted the new Faith, and were baptized. Lydia was apparently a widow, as she was mistress of a household, possessed of considerable property; and she entertained the whole party in her house, pressing her hospitality upon them.

XXVIII

THE FIRST CHRISTIAN CHURCH IN EUROPE

Acts xvi. 16-40

THE conversion of the household of Lydia, and of the jailer in Philippi (which is related subsequently), are examples of the strong family unity that characterized ancient society. House slaves were, as a rule, much attached to their masters, and were regarded as part of the family and as far more trustworthy than hired servants, and the household was governed in a half-patriarchal style. The jailer's household was probably humble and small, yet even he would doubtless have at least one slave. But Lydia's household must have been much larger. She was working a business that required considerable capital, as she was a dealer in a fashionable and rather expensive kind of garments. Her house was able to take in four guests on an unexpected visit; and, though Eastern habits of living are simpler, yet where a woman was the householder, this implies free space and room for separation. The constraint which she applied shows that the four missionaries hesitated to force so large a company on her, and only yielded to her pressing hospitality. The situation also proves that women enjoyed much freedom and respect in those Macedonian cities.

Paul and his friends now had a very favourable opportunity; as he himself would have expressed it, a door was opened to him for work in Philippi. How long he remained there Luke does not define exactly; but there is no reason to think the time was long, or that the evangelization of the city and the formation of the Church were completed by him. That was left to Luke, who remained alone.

The catastrophe was forced on prematurely by a remarkable incident, which is very characteristic of society in the Ægean cities, and which shows what a large part was played by magical and other arts for making money out of the superstitions of the populace. There was a slave-girl who was a skilful ventriloquist, and who gained thereby a considerable income for her masters by pretending to reveal future events and tell fortunes. For the successful practice of such an art it is necessary to possess a certain sensitiveness of temperament; and the girl seems in some subtle way to have appreciated the spiritual influence with which the Apostle and his companions were endowed. Day after day she followed them, calling out " these men are slaves of the Most High God, who proclaim to you a way of salvation ". Now these words, which seem to us to carry some intimation of Christian character, did not convey any such impression to the people in the streets, and there is no reason to think that they were understood in that way by the girl herself. The " Most High God " was a familiar name in the syncretistic paganism of the time, mixed of various Oriental and European elements. " Salvation " was what all were seeking after and asking for in the pagan world, and was often prayed for in pagan votive offerings. Paul seems to have felt that these cries, pursuing him daily, attracted attention to him in a wrong way and were a hindrance to his work; and at last he turned on the girl and addressing the spirit, which according to the ancient idea resided in her, he ordered it to leave her. The spiritual sensitiveness which she really possessed placed her under the influence of a more powerful nature, and from that moment she lost her skill.

The girl's owners, who were thus deprived of an easy livelihood, were extremely annoyed. They evidently conceived the idea that, if the superior influence of the strangers were removed, she might recover her power; and accordingly they brought a charge against the two leaders, Paul and Silas, before the city magistrates. The charge was cleverly contrived to touch the pride of the city, whose glory it was to be Roman and not mere Macedonian like the other towns of the region. The Apostles were accused of causing disorder by trying to introduce customs which were unlawful for the people of Philippi as Romans to practise. Anything that seemed to interfere with or diminish the honour of the city as a Roman Colony roused the indignation of the magistrates. They did not wait to inquire into the grounds of the charge, or the guilt of the accused. The populace rose as one man against these hateful Jews. The magistrates forthwith treated the accusation as proved, and practically condemned Paul and Silas as enemies of the city and of the Empire. They rent their clothes in horror at such abominable acts, and ordered the prisoners to be beaten by the lictors, who, as usual, were in attendance on the magistrates of a Roman city. There was no show of observing Roman law and procedure, merely fussy and pretentious display of loyalty to the Roman name and of horror at the mere accusation of disloyalty. Luke does not mention that friendship for their own citizens, who were injured by strange Jews, played any part in the magistrates' action, but it is not impossible or inconsistent with his narrative that such feelings may have influenced their conduct.

After being beaten Paul and Silas were thrown into prison, and the jailer was specially charged to keep them safe as prisoners of State. At midnight, fastened in the stocks, they were praying and singing hymns, and the prisoners were listening to this strange conduct, when an earthquake occurred. The ill-fitting doors, and the wooden stocks roughly let into the wall, were shaken apart; and the prisoners were thus set at liberty. That strange freaks and accidents of an incalculable and extraordinary kind frequently take place during an earthquake is a fact familiar to every one who has experienced such an event.

The jailer, suddenly awakened to see the doors standing open, and hastily concluding that the prisoners, for whom he was responsible with his life, had taken advantage of the opportunity to escape, was about to kill himself, when Paul called out to him, "do thyself no harm, for we are all here". There must have been light outside, for Paul could see the jailer, but the jailer could not see him. In the dark prison lights were needed (as in XII. 7). Oriental prisons are almost always dark, dirty, noisome, ill-constructed, and badly fitted with appliances for safe custody. When lights were brought, and the jailer was relieved of his anxiety, he was filled with gratitude and respect for the moral and saving power of Paul; and asked about the way of salvation, to which the slave-girl had said that Paul was the guide. In that time of excitement and emotion, the man was more open to belief than in ordinary circumstances. An earthquake is in itself terrifying, the way of suicide had for a moment seemed the only path open to him; and fear was the beginning of wisdom in this as in many other cases. Thus occurred the somewhat sensational and almost melodramatic conclusion of the scene, the conversion of the jailer and his household. Such a conversion, so suddenly brought about, could only be, at best, the beginning of a process of learning the truth, there was much to do before such a man could be raised to the level of Christian life; and here he passes out of our range of knowledge. But Luke, who remained in Philippi, doubtless knew him in the years that followed; and we can conjecture the future from what is here related. This might not unfairly be taken as one of the cases in which Luke, composing his history about A.D. 80, spoke from the point of view and with the outlook that belonged to the age when he was writing.

In the morning the magistrates, having had time to reflect on their hasty conduct, went to the opposite extreme, and sent to release the two prisoners without proceeding further in the case. Paul now claimed the rights of Roman citizens, belonging to himself and Silas (whose proper name was Silvanus), in virtue of which they should have been free from the degradation of personal chastisement. It was now the turn of the magistrates to humble themselves, and the incident at Philippi concludes with their request for pardon and for the departure of these two dangerous men. Apparently Paul considered that it was best to comply with what was practically an order, though put in an apologetic form. His work had been so far successful, and might now be transferred elsewhere, while Luke remained as his representative in charge. It is also possible that the energy and practical experience of Lydia were effective in guiding the development of the first European Church.[1]

Timothy seems either to have gone with Paul and Silas, or to have followed them shortly after (as we gather from XVII. 14).

[1] As has been stated above, the name Lydia was probably only a familiar appellation given in Philippi to this Lydian stranger. In the Epistle to the Philippians she is perhaps one of the two strong-minded ladies, Euodia and Syntyche, who are urged to act in unity in Church work. The familiar use of appellations, or nicknames, or diminutives, was very common in ancient life; and it is characteristic of Paul's more polished manner (see Sect. XXXI) to employ the correct forms, Euodia, Silvanus, Prisca, while Luke speaks in a more familiar way of Lydia, Silas, Priscilla. Such variations show how close both Luke and Paul stand to the persons whom they mention.

XXIX

THE PROGRESS THROUGH MACEDONIA

Acts XVII. 1-15

FROM Philippi Paul and Silas, with Timothy accompanying or following, went along the great Roman road, called the Egnatian Way, to the chief city of the province Macedonia, Thessalonica, which still retains part of its old commercial importance, and its old name in the modified form Salonik. Here there was a settlement of Jews and a Synagogue, where Paul after his usual fashion found an opening for work. On three successive Sabbaths he preached, explaining the real meaning of the Scriptures, and proving that in them the death and resurrection of the Messiah were predicted, and that Jesus had fulfilled these predictions and must therefore be the Messiah.

Some of the Jews believed, especially a man named Jason. Very much greater success, however, was gained among the Hellenic population of the city, both among those called "God-fearing," who had already become accustomed to listen to the lofty teaching of the Jewish Scriptures, and among the ordinary pagans who now for the first time "turned unto God from idols" (1 Thess. i. 9). It is evident, therefore, that besides preaching in the Synagogue, Paul and Silas also taught the ordinary Hellenes of the city in some other way, either during or after the three Sabbaths.

A number of the leading women also cast in their lot with the heralds of the new Faith. Luke makes it a rule to notice how far the teaching of Paul reached the women, who in the circumstances of ancient life had not such ready access to the public lectures of strange teachers, but who were often attracted in private to various forms of Oriental religion, Jewish, Christian, etc. In the Christian assemblies these women found much freer opportunity to give public expression to their views, and thus to strengthen their religious convictions and to affect the opinions of others. But Paul was always cautious and apprehensive lest the Christian women might rouse social disapproval by their freedom, and he was inclined to discourage their open public action, though his principles would not permit him absolutely to forbid a woman whom the Spirit moved to speak.

As elsewhere, so in Thessalonica, the Jews were jealous of this free admission of pagans to equality with themselves, and organized a riot among the low-class and idle mob of the town. They first tried to bring Paul and Silas as strangers before a popular assembly, where the shouting and votes of the mob would influence the proceedings; and, failing to find them, they arraigned Jason and other brethren before the magistrates. A more formal procedure was now required; and they accused their fellow-citizens of having welcomed strangers who were a danger to public order, and of having in concert with them conspired to set up another Emperor, viz. Jesus, and thus been guilty of treason against the rightful Emperor and the Imperial law. This was a skilfully planned charge. At that time treason was interpreted in a wide sense and was very severely punished; anything that could be construed as disrespect to the Emperor was treason, and to speak of another Emperor or King was an unpardonable crime The magistrates were much perturbed, for if they did not treat the charge seriously, they themselves might be accused of disrespect to the Emperor. They took a very lenient course in the circumstances, merely binding the accused to come up for trial when required; and the brethren sent Paul and Silas away to Beroea. This proceeding, taken in conjunction with Paul's statement that he was hindered by Satan from returning to Thessalonica

(1 Thess. II. 18), implies that Jason and the rest would be tried if Paul returned to trouble the city, but would remain unharmed so long as Paul was kept out. In this ingenious way the magistrates saved their own fellow-citizens, and pacified the accusers, whose object was to get rid of Paul and Silas.

The magistrates of Philippi and Thessalonica are called by their correct titles, strategoi and politarchai, and the people of the latter city are rightly called Hellenes, a name which the Roman Colony Philippi would have rejected. All these and many other little details show the minute accuracy of Luke.

This premature departure from Thessalonica greatly disturbed Paul. The congregation was not sufficiently instructed to be safely left to itself. His anxiety to return, and the need that there was to clear away from the minds of the Thessalonians some mistakes which they were making as to the meaning of his teaching, are shown in his two letters to them, written very shortly after his departure. These letters are unique in their anxious and special care of an infant congregation.

Paul had been driven from Philippi even more unexpectedly and prematurely, yet he felt no such anxiety in that case, but in later years recalls with grateful memory the conduct of the Philippian

Church in the months that followed his departure. The difference was, certainly, due to the fact that Luke remained in charge there, but no one was left at Thessalonica to whom Paul could so implicitly trust. Hence he had to send Timothy and Silas, when he found it impossible himself to return. Yet, while he was anxious about the Thessalonians, Paul in his letters finds no fault with them, but extols in the highest terms their noble conduct, which made them a pattern to all. He tactfully praises them for the steadfastness which he desired to encourage in them.

Paul and his company went on to the inland Macedonian town of Beroea, and there found a kindly welcome and an attentive audience in the Synagogue In this remote Macedonian town the Jews were probably isolated, and gladly received the visit of men of their own nation, and without any prejudice examined carefully the evidence which Paul pointed out in the Prophets about the Coming and the Life of the Messiah. Many of them believed in the new teaching, and with them were associated a considerable number of Hellenes, especially ladies. Considering the marked favour shown to Paul in this Synagogue, we may safely consider that the Beroean Church consisted largely of Jews and the "God-fearing" Hellenes, who had already come under the attractive and im-

XXIX. THE PROGRESS THROUGH MACEDONIA

pressive influence of the Hebrew monotheism: these were the most thoughtful and serious part of the Hellenes, possessed of a naturally religious mind.

But the enmity of the Jews in Thessalonica still pursued Paul. They sent agents who roused the Beroean populace to disorder; and the brethren, fearing further riots, sent Paul away, convoyed by certain of themselves, down to the sea-coast. Here there occurred apparently some change of plan, for the Beroean delegates ultimately brought Paul to Athens, and came back with a message to Silas and Timothy bidding them join him there. It would seem that his intention had been to sail back to Thessalonica, but that such news reached him as to prevent this plan from being put in execution (1 Thess. II. 18). There was no legal power preventing his return to Thessalonica, but only the evil consequences to Jason and his friends; and there was every hope that after a time, when the acuteness of the situation had quieted down so far as the magistrates were concerned, it might be possible for him to rejoin his infant Church. The change of plan had to be notified to his co-adjutors. Apparently the plan was that Silas and Timothy should take Thessalonica on their way to Athens, and do what Paul was prevented from doing.

The completeness and perfection with which the narrative in Acts is illustrated by, and throws light in its turn on, the Thessalonian letters, makes the study of the relations between them exceptionally instructive.

XXX

PAUL AT ATHENS

Acts xvii. 16-34

PAUL'S experiences in Athens are in some ways the most picturesque and interesting incident in his whole career. He found himself in the city which was the centre and the originator of Greek University life and education; and, as one who was trained at Tarsus in the learning of the Greeks, he surveyed the city, its buildings and sights (such is the force of the verb in verse 16), and was roused to indignation that it was full of idols.

Besides his ordinary custom of preaching in the Synagogue to the Jews and the God-fearing pagans who resorted thither, he adapted himself to the Athenian manner, and discussed philosophical subjects and the nature of God in the market-place, as Socrates and other thinkers had done, with any chance person. In this way he came into relations with some philosophers of the two schools, which at that time were eminent in Greek philosophic circles, the Stoic and the Epicurean.

In the theory of the Stoic school, man was the master of his fate and supreme in himself, not dependent on God, but seeking for himself after virtue and finding in it the highest good. The Epicureans enjoined as the aim and rule of life to enjoy in soul-quietness as many as possible of the higher pleasures and nobler sensations of human nature, especially the mental emotions, apart from any relation to God. Practically, both philosophies made man and not God the ruler of life; and this denial of Divine government issued in making the city of philosophers also the city where idols were most numerous Those who made light of God were willing to accept and recognize any number of gods. When Paul spoke of Jesus and the Resurrection, the Athenians thought he was talking about two foreign deities whose worship he wished to introduce.

In the heat of discussion, while some called him contemptuously a mere vulgar plagiarist and stealer of other men's ideas (referring to the obvious and intentional analogies between many of Paul's statements and those of pagan philosophers), they at last took hold of him and brought him before Areopagus, the court which had some kind of charge of public morals and teaching, and which took its name from the hill where originally it had sat to try cases of murder, though it had long since changed its seat and its jurisdiction. In the court the question was formally put to Paul, what was this new teaching which he was setting forth, and the desire was expressed to know its exact nature. Thus before the highest moral and educational tribunal of the ancient world Paul was placed by his opponents to state his message to the Greek world.

The occasion was dramatic, and Luke fully appreciated the effectiveness of the situation. There is a subtle difference of tone here in the narrative corresponding to his conception of the scene as a whole. At this point he places his report, once for all, of the message which Paul brought to the pagans. At Pisidian Antioch he gave the report of Paul's address to a mixed audience of Jews and God-fearing Gentiles; but he reserved for the centre of Greek education his account of the way in which Paul introduced his doctrine to an entirely ignorant and unprepared assembly in a Hellenic city. There is no reason to think that the speech was radically different in tone from the kind of introductory addresses which he might have used to purely pagan audiences in other cities. It is more philosophic in expression, corresponding to the different standard of education in the hearers, but otherwise it is probably on the same religious plane.

Paul treats the worship of deities by the pagans as a misdirected form of a right and natural religious impulse; that Divine power which they worshipped wrongly in ignorance Paul declared to them in its true form. The true God, who made the world and gives all good things to mankind (XIV. 15, 17), is immaterial and spiritual, standing in need of nothing from men; therefore the principle of paganism, that men build houses for God to dwell in and give Him gifts to make Him kindly disposed to them, is false. It is not the case that each nation has its separate deity, but the one God has made all mankind one in obedience to himself, and His intention is that men should seek after Him and find Him, who is close to man, and who is the guiding Power in all things and the life of all men. As the pagan poets, Aratus and Cleanthes, have said, " We are also His offspring ". Since we are God's children, we should not think that God our Father resembles any image of gold or silver or stone, carved by human art, for He is purely spiritual and ideal. In the former times God left man to learn from those natural witnesses of himself, viz the good things which He gives to all.[1] But now He has sent a special message of repent-

[1] These words should be compared with the similar, but more simply expressed, sentiment in the remonstrance addressed to the mob at Lystra (Acts XIV.).

ance. This opportunity for repentance from the errors and sins of paganism must be used immediately, for the Judgment is coming, and God has appointed a Man to come and judge the world according to the opportunities offered to it; the proof that the message is true lies in the fact that God raised from the dead the Man whom He sent.

This speech was addressed primarily to the Areopagus, but largely to the general audience who stood round the judges and the parties. In ancient life and even in courts of law the audience played a very important part. Lawyers pleading a case often addressed themselves to the crowd instead of the judges; and the applause or disapproval of the audience represented the public verdict on intellectual displays.

In Athens Paul was understood to be one of those new teachers who so often came there to try and win fame and fortune by their gifts of rhetoric or dialectic; and the audience regarded his speech mainly with the curiosity of idlers whose chief interest lay in telling or hearing some new thing. They flocked to hear this supposed new aspirant for intellectual distinction, but what they expected from such a person was a brilliant literary performance. The intense earnestness of Paul touched no corresponding chord in their hearts, but roused in some only a feeling of contempt and expressions of mockery, while others said more politely but probably quite as carelessly, that they would hear him again on some future occasion. The more or less highly educated audience in the hall of Areopagus was the most difficult in the world for a preacher of religion to address; and there can be no doubt that Luke marks this by his rather contemptuous description of them (verses 21, 32), and by his statement that Paul "went forth from the midst of them". Not much success attended his work in Athens, and no Church seems to have been formed there at this time.

Yet even among these idle and frivolous loungers, priding themselves on their culture and their superiority to vulgar emotions and ideas, there were some who caught the ring of genuineness and truth in Paul's words. One member of the Areopagus and a woman named Damaris and a few others became adherents of the new teaching. Damaris is not said to belong (as the converted women in Beroea and Thessalonica did) to the higher circle of society. Athenian usage precluded women of the better class from being present at discussions in the market-place or a formal discourse before the Areopagus. It is a striking feature in Luke's character, and shows also the exactness of his knowledge, that he records the conversion and the name of this woman side by side with the noble Areopagite Dionysius.

Paul himself seems to have recognized that speculative philosophy was a poor preparation for a religious training; and in Corinth, his next centre of work, he "determined not to know anything save Jesus Christ and Him crucified" (1 Cor. II. 2); and his simple kind of preaching there was contrasted by some of the Corinthian Christians unfavourably with the more philosophic style of Apollos. But, whatever may have been the variation in Paul's style from the Athenian speech with its quotation from versified philosophy, the substance and the basis of his teaching was everywhere the same.

XXXI

THE CHARTER OF CHRISTIAN FREEDOM IN THE ROMAN EMPIRE

Acts XVIII. 1-18

PAUL, when he sent directions to Silas and Timothy to join him in Athens, apparently intended to stay there for some time. He found, however, that the place and the people were not readily accessible: "there was not an open door" in the great University town; society was too self-complacent, too clever after a fashion, too critical with regard to style and outward form. Paul therefore departed from Athens, and went to Corinth, the metropolis of the Roman province, an ancient and famous city, the greatest centre of trade and exchange in Greece from the beginning of Greek history onwards.

Corinth had been totally destroyed by the Romans when they conquered Greece in 146 B.C., but had forthwith risen afresh from its ashes, and re-established itself as the commercial centre of the Greek world. On the narrow isthmus which divided two seas, it was planted on the direct line of communication between Rome and the East. Travellers and officials avoided, in general, the unbroken sea-route round the south end of Greece; and sailed to the one side of the isthmus, spent some days in Corinth, and then sailed again from the other coast on their further course from or to Rome. Much trade also followed this course, preferring the trouble and expense of transhipment at the isthmus to the risks of coasting round the ill-famed promontory Malea, which was proverbial as a danger to the small vessels of the ancients, though it presents no terror to modern ships. If Athens was the intellectual capital of the world, the city of art and of the higher civilization, Corinth was the capital of the province Achaia and the centre of life in the Ægean world, a Roman Colony like Philippi and Lystra, looking westwards and eastwards along the great route of the Empire to Italy and Rome on the one side, to Ephesus and all Asia on the other.

Such a commanding point was precisely the sort of place which Paul found most useful in his work. In Philippi and Thessalonica he had been working along the land-road between Rome and the East; but the central and far most important line of communication was that which passed through Corinth. The situation of all these cities throws light on the inner purpose which was working itself out in Paul's mind and life. How far he was himself conscious of it as yet, or how far the Spirit was working in him without his full comprehension, we cannot say. After no long time we find him looking forward to Rome itself as his goal (Acts XIX. 21). But from the first start he had been groping in a vague way along the sea-road (XIII. 4-13) and the land-road leading towards the capital of the world.

In Corinth Paul found two persons who were destined to play a considerable part in early Christian history, though we can only dimly guess what they did. In A.D. 50 the Emperor Claudius had expelled the Jews from Rome. Such attempts had been made more than once before, but all proved unsuccessful; it was as easy to stop the incoming tide on the seashore as to prevent the Jews from collecting at the centre of the world's financial operations, where money was most plentiful and commerce at its busiest. For the moment many Jews had to retire, but soon the edict fell into disuse and they came back. On account of this edict Aquila, a Jew of Pontus, and his wife Prisca (commonly known, as here, by the diminutive form Priscilla, cp. Rom. XVI. 3), had come from Rome to Corinth early in A.D. 51. Prisca was probably a Roman lady of good birth, as she is often mentioned before her husband. Paul uses the more formal and polite name Prisca (as he does Silvanus). Luke always employs the familiar form which he was accustomed to hear in everyday life, Priscilla (so also he speaks of Silas). Such little touches are very characteristic of the two men. Paul had the high courtesy of the true aristocrat even in the small matters of life. His friendship with Prisca and Aquila probably caused his Roman plans to come rapidly to maturity in his mind. He learned from them the condition of Rome.

The readiness with which Paul and the two exiles joined company is explained partly by their common trade, but a stronger reason must have been that the strangers from Rome were sympathetic, in other words that they were already inclined towards the Faith of the Messiah. Whether they were already Christians cannot be determined, as Luke is silent; but, if they were, they had learned only in a very imperfect way from the informal teaching of Jews at Rome, and their friendship with Paul must have produced a powerful effect on their understanding of the Faith. Who could live with Paul in close companionship and not be strongly influenced? Some Jews hated Paul; others would give their life for him; none could remain indifferent or preserve mere formal and commonplace relations with him.

As usual, Paul began with public addresses in the Synagogue to the Jews and the Hellenes [1] who had already come in some degree under the influence of the Jewish faith. When Silas and Timothy came from Macedonia to join him, he devoted himself entirely to preaching, showing to the Jews that the Messiah whom they expected was that Jesus who had already lived and been crucified. As in other places, a party was soon formed against Paul among the Jews, feeling grew unusually bitter; and Luke describes the situation in exceptionally strong terms. Paul retired from the Synagogue, and turned his attention to the general pagan population. He found a place of meeting next door to the Synagogue in the house of a Roman citizen, Titius Justus.[2] This juxtaposition was not calculated to sweeten the relations with the Jewish opposition, and legal proceedings soon ensued. But in the meantime Paul was encouraged in a vision to persevere in his work.

[1] Hellenes in Corinth are the natives of Hellas (Greece) as distinguished from the Roman citizens who formed the aristocracy of the Colony. Hellenes in the Asian and other cities outside of Hellas were generally natives educated in Greek manners (Section IX).

[2] His name was in full probably Gaius Titius Justus, the Gaius of Rom. XVI. 23.

206 XXXI. THE CHARTER OF CHRISTIAN FREEDOM

Such messages from God come to the man who is wholly absorbed in his work, and is eager to find and follow the Divine guidance.

Some of the Jews, including a chief of the Synagogue named Crispus, believed and were baptized; the last duty was as a rule left by Paul to his coadjutors and subordinates like Timothy. The practical work of keeping a congregation together by a regular system of ritual was never undervalued by the great Apostle (as appears, e.g., in 1 Tim. II. 1-8); but he could leave this part of congregational duty to others, while he devoted himself wholly to what others could not do like him, viz. the evangelistic work.

The recalcitrant Jews brought a charge against Paul before the Roman Governor of the province, Junius Gallio, a brother of the famous philosopher and statesman Seneca; but they did not show such skill in attack as those of Thessalonica. They accused him of persuading men to worship God contrary to the Law. Gallio decided forthwith against them, refusing to listen to their case; he declared that in a charge of misdemeanour or crime he was ready to hear evidence, but in a matter of religion and ritual the Roman State would not interfere. When the Jews were thus expelled from the court the Gentile crowd, which always disliked them, seized Sosthenes, a ruler of the Synagogue,[1] and beat him, while Gallio took no notice of this ebullition of public feeling.

The decision of the Governor was most important. It amounted to a declaration of freedom in religious teaching; the Christians might preach, and the Roman State would not interfere with them, unless they were charged with some breach of the civil or criminal law. Thus Rome became for a time the protector of the new teaching against Jewish opposition. A decision by an official of high standing tended to become a precedent guiding the judgment of others, although in itself it did not necessarily constitute a rule. Seneca's spirit was similar to Gallio's; and, as Seneca was now and for some years later one of the leading spirits in Roman administration, this decision of his brother was almost a charter of freedom to the Church, until the higher tribunal of the Empire overruled it a good many years later.

The time when Gallio governed the province Achaia has been determined by a recent inscription [2] as A.D. 52 (probably from spring 52 to spring 53). Paul resided in Corinth eighteen months, and then went to Cæsarea (and Jerusalem), doubtless for

[1] Sosthenes became a Christian afterwards (1 Cor. I. 1). Some, however, understand that he was already a Christian, and that it was the Jews who took and beat him.

[2] Found at Delphi, in the French excavations.

the Passover. He therefore resided in Corinth from about September 51 to February or March 53. The chronology of his second journey, then, is as follows. He left Syrian Antioch in early spring 50; spent April-May in Syria and Cilicia, summer in South Galatia, autumn in the long wandering that ended at last in Philippi; the winter of 50-51 in Philippi and chiefly in Thessalonica; summer of 51 in Beroea, which he left about the end of July or early August; the journey to Athens and Corinth and a brief residence in Athens filled up the month of August and perhaps a week or two more.

Note—The reason why Paul is not said in Acts XVIII 22 to have gone up from Cæsarea to Jerusalem may have been that by some accident he arrived in Cæsarea too late for the Feast. Sailing ships could not count on their voyage as accurately as modern steamers, and even steamers sometimes have a breakdown. Compare his anxiety on a later voyage as to arriving in time (Acts XX. 16). That he was going to the Feast, according to the Received Text and Authorized Version of XVIII. 21, seems beyond doubt; but the reference to the Feast was omitted in several of the best manuscripts by a correction, which was intended to harmonize verses 21 and 22.

XXXII

ADVICE TO A NEWLY FORMED CHURCH

1 *Thess.* v. 12-24

THE first letter to the congregation at Thessalonica, the earliest Epistle of Paul that has been preserved, was written shortly after Paul had settled in Corinth, upon the arrival of Timothy, who had gone back to Thessalonica to discharge some urgent duties which Paul's sudden departure had prevented. Among these we may probably reckon the appointment of presbyters.

The situation at Thessalonica was similar to that which existed in the three Galatian cities, Antioch, Iconium, Lystra, at the time when Paul had been suddenly expelled from them. He himself returned to them to give them a constitution by the election of presbyters and by other arrangements. He was eager to return in the same way to Thessalonica, but was prevented (as has been said above) by the power of evil; and he sent word to Timothy to go from Beroea to Thessalonica and there do what

Paul did personally in the Galatian cities (Acts XIV. 21 f.; 1 Thess. III. 2 f.). Silas, we may presume, remained on in Beroea for a similar purpose, and returned along with Timothy, probably through Thessalonica. The history as narrated in Acts and the references contained in the Epistle complete one another.

The letter, and especially the concluding chapter of it, show what he thought most important to impress upon this congregation, recently formed, inexperienced, and still far from firmly established in morality, good conduct, and the understanding of what true religion means and requires, and of what is calculated to build up a firm religious foundation for a good life.

The earlier part of the letter is concerned with matters about which Timothy had brought a report to Paul—matters which might not necessarily happen in every congregation; but the conclusion is universal advice, equally suitable to all persons young in the Faith, and briefly summing up Paul's views as to the practical working of a young congregation. The order in which he states the various points that need to be emphasized and impressed on the Thessalonian congregation is in itself significant; and they must be noted successively as Paul mentions them.

1. You should understand thoroughly the char-

acter of the officials who have been chosen to manage the Church. Their duties are threefold : (1) to work in the congregation ; (2) to rule over and represent it in a religious point of view (i.e. in the Lord); (3) to teach and preach. These duties are not apportioned, some to one class of officials, some to another; each official takes part in all three, though, naturally, each would tend to give himself most to the department which proved most suitable to his talents and bent of mind. The officials are to be regarded with loving respect and esteem by reason of their work—not simply because of their official rank, but because of what they are doing among you.

That this should be the first point which Paul takes up is highly significant. It shows what stress he laid on good administration and good government in the Church. A well-governed Church will be more effective, more vigorous, sounder and more moral; that is Luke's view as shown throughout the Acts, and it is Paul's (as appears also in other letters, and especially those to Timothy and Titus).

2. In your relations with one another, live peaceably, teach and correct those who do not keep step and order in the march of the Church, cheer those who have lost courage, hold up with your help those who are weak and likely to fall, but in every

case make great allowance for all, and do not be impatient with their faults and failings. Never try to revenge yourselves on one another by returning evil for evil and "tit for tat," but always try to find opportunities of doing good to each other and to all the world.

After the duty of the congregation to the officials, Paul here sums up the duty of the members to one another, and the whole is an expansion in detail of the one universal law "that ye love one another". It is particularly important that the duty of teaching, which has just been assigned to the officials, is here prescribed for all members of the congregation; the same work is suitable for both officials and ordinary persons; the same Greek word "teach" is used in respect of both; the idea had not as yet arisen that there existed any separate order of clergy, charged with the duty of teaching. Every member of the congregation may have occasion to teach and admonish. But, whereas the officials are charged permanently and regularly with this duty, the ordinary members only perform the duty in special cases, where they see a fault or a weakness and are able to correct it, and wherever some special call is apparent.

The Greek word which is rendered "disorderly" contains a metaphor which afterwards became widely used; the Christian life is the march of the Christian army, in which all must keep step and rank unbroken.

In the last detail which is mentioned it is urged on these newly converted pagans that they must seek every opportunity of doing a kindness to those outside the Church in the pagan world as well as to Christians. The old pagan idea was that the benefits of the common religion ought to be confined to those who had the right of membership, and should not be given to others, as if there were only a limited total so that the share of each would be diminished if the number of participants was enlarged. The Christian should follow after that which is good toward all.

3. Paul next mentions one's duty to oneself. Be always full of the joy of true religion; make your life a continuous uninterrupted prayer; be grateful in every part of life, for God especially desires to see in you a spirit of thankfulness.

4 There has been as yet no allusion to the duty of assembling together in public worship. This topic is now introduced; but, in consequence of the still unregulated and unformed conditions of public worship, Paul does not mention the manner and the ritual, but only the action of the Divine Spirit in the congregation. This action was manifested most in the public assembly, but also appeared in other ways, in sporadic inspiration of

individuals, and in the heart of each Christian. The fire of inspiration and enthusiasm should never be damped down by cold treatment and ridicule or contempt. Especially the inspired utterances which were often heard in those early congregations must not be despised On the other hand one must not accept as inspired every utterance that was ecstatic and unusual; many of them were the result of mental excitement, not of real inspiration; all must be carefully tested before they are accepted as caused by the action of the Spirit; everything that is good and has stood the test should be grasped and retained as a permanent possession for the Church. In testing these utterances the rule may be confidently followed to abstain from and reject every kind of evil. If an ecstatic utterance conflicts in any way whatsoever with anything that we know to be good, it may safely be dismissed as uninspired and resulting from mere mental excitation.

This series of rules is concluded with the prayer that God, who gives the peace that is invoked for the Thessalonians in the opening verse, may make them perfect and pure in their whole nature, spirit and soul and body. The God who has called each of you into the Church will do this for you; the fact that He has called you is the guarantee that He will complete His work.

XXXIII

THE IMPERIAL AIMS OF PAUL

Acts XVIII. 23–XIX. 22

PAUL'S third journey from Antioch began with another survey of the Galatian Churches, his earliest Gentile congregations, which were always a special care to him. Then he proceeded to Ephesus, the capital of Asia, the great city on the eastern shore of the Ægean Sea, looking across the sea westwards towards Corinth and Rome, while it was the end of many roads which came from the East and converged here at the harbour from which travellers sailed towards the capital of the Roman Empire. Thus at last he carried into effect the intention which he had in mind, when he was leaving Galatia on his second journey, and which the Spirit had forbidden (Acts XVI. 7).

At Ephesus the new religion had already planted itself, but only in an imperfect form, which is called by Luke "the baptism of John": it was a teaching which concerned itself with the Messiah, and regarded Jesus as having fulfilled the Messianic prophecies, but which apparently failed to comprehend the purpose of Jesus' death and the power of the Cross in the salvation of mankind. It did not, therefore, carry with it that intensity of enthusiasm and that burning fire of belief, which was recognized by the early Christians as the gift of the Holy Spirit.

Priscilla and Aquila, who had left Corinth along with Paul, settled in Ephesus while he went to Cæsarea and Antioch; and they exerted some influence in making known the Gospel as Paul taught it. Especially this was the case in regard to a learned and eloquent Jew from Alexandria, named Apollos, who came and preached the baptism of John in Ephesus. They instructed this man more carefully in the Way of the Lord, as they had learned it from Paul. When Apollos was going on a missionary tour to Corinth, they gave him letters to the Church there; and his work was very effective in the great city of Achaia, both in helping the Christians and in confuting the Jews by proving from the Prophecies of the Old Testament that Jesus was the Messiah.

Luke's purpose in dwelling on this episode is to show that even Apollos's teaching at Corinth was Pauline in character and owed its effectiveness largely to the ideas of Paul learned through Paul's two disciples. We, who are accustomed to regard Paul's teaching as the chief power in spreading the new Faith, realize only with an effort the circumstances amid which Luke wrote his history, when the effectiveness and value of Paul's work was the subject of sharp discussion, and when many declared that the learned and philosophical preaching of Apollos had done more in Corinth than Paul's teaching, and that there was a Christian congregation in Ephesus before Paul went there. Accordingly, Luke shows also that these early Ephesian disciples, real Christians in a sense, had neither received nor heard about the Holy Spirit until Paul came; and it was through the laying of Paul's hands on them that they received the supreme gift.

The Jews in Ephesus were less hostile at first than in most cities; and Paul preached in the Synagogue for three months, an unusually long period of friendliness. Then hostility arose, and the Apostle had to leave the Synagogue and go direct to the Gentiles, making the lecture-room of Tyrannus his centre, where every day he taught for five hours, from one hour before midday till two hours before sunset; in the earlier part of the day the room was used for other purposes, i.e. doubtless for the teaching of Tyrannus himself.

Two years were spent in this kind of work; and,

as Ephesus was the commercial capital of the Roman province Asia, and was visited for trade and other reasons by great numbers from other Asian centres, every city in the province was affected to some degree, and congregations were formed in places like Colossae, Hierapolis and Laodicea, which Paul did not himself visit. Probably some of his coadjutors and subordinates visited these and other cities, while Paul himself preached to the great mixed audiences in Ephesus.

The effect produced was evidently very great, both on the listeners and on Paul himself. In the first place his plans grew wider and more imperial, as he became more clearly conscious of the possibilities of the situation in the Roman world; and Luke marks the growing clearness and breadth of Paul's outlook, by placing at this point his first statement of the boldness and all-embracing nature of his plans. He "spoke boldly". As Luke has already described his preaching in so many Gentile cities, there was some special reason why he emphasizes the boldness of Paul's preaching in Ephesus. Further, Luke describes Paul's great scheme, first to complete the evangelization of the two provinces, Macedonia and Achaia, by personal work, then after visiting Jerusalem to go to Rome and mould the character of the infant Church there, as he had affected the views and character of the disciples whom he found in Ephesus.

The brief statement about Jerusalem contains an essential part of Paul's purpose, which was apparently so well known to the readers of Luke's work that it is not formally mentioned by him, but only casually alluded to here and in XXIV. 17. Yet, by comparison with Paul's own letters, we gather what was its nature. The new Pauline Churches were scattered over the four provinces, Galatia, Asia, Macedonia, and Achaia. The ensuing visit to the last two would complete his work for the present in the eastern lands, and the visit to Jerusalem was to be the climax and end of that work; and thereafter he would no longer go about among them preaching the Kingdom (xx. 25), but would devote himself to work in Rome and in the West (Rom. xv. 24).

It was, however, essential to his designs that the four provinces should be closely knit in unity and brotherhood to the central Church at Jerusalem. In Syrian Antioch that end had been attained largely through the kindness and the help shown by the new to the original Church (XI. 29 f.). We have described in a previous lesson the importance of this act. Paul was now again applying the same method. First in the Galatian Churches, then in the others, he instituted a weekly collection, the proceeds of which were to be carried to Jerusalem by delegates representing the four provinces, as a testimony of the fraternal feeling that bound together all the scattered parts of the one Universal Church. Such was the bold and statesmanlike plan which the great Apostle was working out.

In the second place, the marvellous power which was exercised by Paul over the minds and souls and bodies of those with whom he came into relation is described in striking terms. Numerous cases of healing, which belong to the category of faith-cure, occurred; and the Apostle was brought into direct antagonism with the magicians and others who practised on the superstitions of the vulgar to gain a livelihood. As in other cases already mentioned at Samaria, Paphos and Philippi, these magicians possessed a certain amount of real knowledge and of the power which knowledge gives, and this they eked out by arts of imposture. As before, the influence of the cheat and the charlatan yielded to the sublime power of true faith and true knowledge. Some impostors attempted to use the power of Paul by appealing to "the Jesus whom Paul preacheth," and were signally discomfited. The idea in their minds was similar to that which had impelled Simon of Samaria to buy from Peter and John a share of their knowledge and power. There is a generic resemblance, amid differences of detail, in all these encounters between the new Faith and the practisers of magic; and their frequency shows how powerful an influence was exerted on the society of that period by such persons, who combined a certain amount of skill and knowledge with the arts of the charlatan and impostor.

XXXIV

PAUL'S VICTORY OVER THE MOB IN EPHESUS

Acts xix. 23–xx. 1

THE catastrophe which interrupted Paul's work in Ephesus came at last after two years and three months' residence (called three years, xx. 31, according to the universal ancient custom of reckoning two years and a fraction as three years). It was brought about not, as usual, through the Jews, but through the Hellenes. In Ephesus there was evidently good feeling on the part of some Jews towards the new Faith, and Jewish opposition did not go to any serious extreme.

Ephesus was the seat of the worship of the goddess Artemis, who was reverenced by visitors from the whole province Asia as deeply as by the citizens themselves. Her worshippers, whether native to the city or coming from other places, used to buy and dedicate in the temple or carry to their own homes images of the goddess in her shrine. According to their means these shrines were of silver, or marble, or stone, or terra-cotta, more or less ornamental and expensive. There were images to suit all purses. The fabrication of these shrines (*naoi*, as they were called) was a trade of importance in the city, giving employment to a large number of workmen. Those who worked in an expensive material, like silver, needed more capital, belonged to a higher social grade, and applied a higher standard of art in their work. The whole business was organized as a trade-guild, like almost every trade in Asia Minor, and the guild of "shrine-makers" was very influential in the city. Hundreds of such shrines are found in all parts of the provinces of Asia and Galatia. The silver shrines, naturally, have all perished; but the less valuable ones remain in great numbers.

The teaching of Paul had produced such effect in the city that the shrine-makers' sales were seriously diminished. People were listening to Paul instead of buying and dedicating shrines. The guild became alarmed about the future of their industry. The case was typical of what often occurs in the development of civilization and the elevation of the moral standard of society. Trades which minister to the lower tastes of the populace dwindle and die: the workmen employed in these trades are thrown out of employment: these men are often not individually worse than other tradespeople: they do the work they were brought up to do, and take no more thought about what effect they are producing on society than other workmen: they merely earn their daily bread in the line of trade open to them. What is to be done in such a situation? The tradesmen in Ephesus answered this question by raising an outcry against the new order of things. Civilization and progress must give way to the interests of the workmen and the employers. A maker of silver shrines named Demetrius, a leading man in the trade, called a meeting of the craftsmen, and pointed out the loss to their trading profits, and the impiety and danger to the religion of the city, which resulted from Paul's teaching. This Paul (as he said) was affecting seriously not only Ephesus, but almost the whole of the province. The prospect of such loss to themselves and to their goddess roused a storm of indignation; the city was thrown into confusion; crowds rushed through the streets and flocked into the great theatre, seizing and taking with them two of Paul's companions, Gaius and Aristarchus.

This incidental allusion throws light on the Apostle's methods: we may take it as certain that he often had with him, especially in his later years, a number of companions to help in his work: Timothy, whom he chose at Lystra, is one example of many such associates added to the small company which started from Antioch: Luke himself and Gaius and Aristarchus are examples of the same class. Gaius belonged to Derbe, Aristarchus to Thessalonica.

Paul wished to go into the theatre and address the crowd, but his friends dissuaded him; and some of the Asiarchs who were friendly to him sent messages begging him not to run such a risk. The Asiarchs were officials of the province, whose duty was to regulate the rites and ceremonies of the Imperial religion (i.e. the worship of the Emperors, living and dead, as embodiments in human form of the Divine power that guarded and guided the whole Roman Empire). The fact that the Asiarchs helped Paul shows that at this time the Roman government in the Eastern provinces was not unfavourable to free religious teaching. The attitude of Gallio at Corinth and of Sergius Paulus at Paphos points to the same conclusion.

The Jews of Ephesus were afraid that they might be involved in the same danger as Paul their fellow-countryman, and they put forward one of their people, named Alexander, to speak on their behalf and clear them of complicity in Paul's action; but when the crowd became aware that he was a Jew, they would not listen to him. The mob of Greek cities always hated the Jews, though a number of thoughtful Hellenes were attracted to the pure and lofty morality of the Jewish faith. The meeting was now a scene of utter disorder: many who had rushed with the crowd did not know why the assembly had come together: for two hours all continued to shout in honour of "Great Artemis of the Ephesians".

At last the secretary of the city, a municipal official of great importance, who was charged beyond any other with managing the delicate relation between the Imperial government and the municipal administration, succeeded in obtaining a hearing. He humoured the crowd by stating in the first place that the city derived its special honour from being the guardian of the goddess and of her temple; that was a fact indisputable, and there was no reason for alarm, as if the goddess or her worship were in danger. But as to the two men whom the mob had dragged into the theatre, they had not been guilty of treason to the Empire ("robbers of temples" is a mere mistranslation) or of disrespect to the religion of the city. If Demetrius and the trade-guild of which he was a leading member had any ground of complaint against them, there was justice to be had in the regular courts of law; an accusation ought to be lodged in the regular way. If issues of a wider kind, touching the relation of these strangers to the municipality, were involved, such matters ought to come before a regular meeting of the public assembly, but an irregular gathering like the present was illegal and amounted to a riot. The Imperial government was always suspicious of popular assemblies, and apprehensive lest they might try to meddle in matters beyond their sphere; and there was great risk lest the city should be involved in trouble on account of the disorderly proceedings of the day.

After listening to this sharp rebuke, the meeting dispersed Paul had triumphed, and his enemies were discomfited. The leading official in the city had pronounced him and his friends innocent in respect of the graver matters of treason against the Roman State or disrespect to the religious establishment of the city. The Asiarchs, all men of the highest standing, representing the educated pagan world, had taken a lively interest in saving him from danger: they were, as a rule, men who had held other municipal priesthoods before attaining the supreme priestly office, and it was one of the strangely ironical facts of the whole situation that the priests should help the man who was most bent on destroying their ritual. But paganism was not exclusive; and pagans rarely objected to the introduction of a new god into the Pantheon.

XXXIV. VICTORY OVER THE MOB IN EPHESUS

Luke does not lay stress on the troubles and dangers which Paul had to face in Ephesus; but from the Apostle's words to the Corinthians we know that his residence there was a time of great anxiety. The result of the riot was that Paul, who had intended to stay in Ephesus until Pentecost, A D. 56, left the city earlier in the year, and went by Troas into Macedonia and Achaia. Since he left Corinth in spring 53, he had gone to Cæsarea, Jerusalem, and Antioch; he stayed in Antioch a short time, wrote there the Epistle to the Galatians, and afterwards travelled through the Galatian Churches in autumn and early winter 53.

XXXV

A HYMN OF LOVE THE DIVINE

1 *Cor.* XIII. 1-13

WHILE Paul was never afraid to speak in the strongest and sharpest condemnation, if need were, of some serious fault in any of his congregations as a whole, or of any crime committed by an individual, the method of blame was not that which he most commonly practised in his letters. He used more frequently the method of praise. Sometimes he encouraged his converts to struggle on along the difficult path of progress by praising them for doing that which he wished them to do, when he could see any signs of their attempting already to do it. Also he frequently lauded highly a virtue in which those to whom he was writing were markedly deficient, without saying or even hinting that they were lacking. The correction and improvement of his pupils was always his object, and he used every possible means of attaining this end; but it was most akin to his nature to encourage them, and it wounded him to be forced to blame or to condemn.

In this case, when he was writing to the Corinthians, he perceived clearly that one quality was most lacking in them and most needful for their improvement; and he devotes one of the most wonderful and exquisite chapters in all his letters to the praise of the quality which he calls *agape*, and which the Authorized Version renders "charity," while the Revised Version prefers the translation "Love". Neither term is a quite satisfactory equivalent to Paul's word; but "love" is as near the truth as our language can come. We need more "agape," and our speech fails to express exactly the full force of the quality which we lack. Every nation needs more love. It is the quality which Jesus meant, when He gave the order to "love thy neighbour as thyself"; it embraces the most comprehensive and strongest kind of good-will to all men, a deep and burning desire to seek after the progress of the race and the benefit of every individual with whom we are brought into relations; it is entirely unselfish; it develops the side of our own nature in which we can approximate nearest to the Divine nature, because it is the human counterpart of the feeling that God entertains to man.

Now it is evident throughout the letter that this

quality was one in which the Corinthians were distinctly lacking. Every one who studies ancient Greek history or the modern Greek people recognizes that it is on this side that the Greeks especially require to improve. They have many excellent qualities, but these are mostly on the side of acuteness, intelligent comprehension of personal advantage, and desire to give free play to their individual nature and character; and as a race they need to be developed on the altruistic side. In the Corinthian congregation such were the qualities that Paul observed—qualities which in moderate degree are good and useful, but which very easily grow too strong and become dangerous and even faulty, unless constantly controlled and directed by the supreme power of Love, whose praise Paul sings in a prose poem of marvellous beauty. The Corinthians were eagerly desirous to attain excellence, to be pre-eminent in good and brilliant qualities, to be wise and philosophical, to understand the world in which they lived, to criticize and correct their neighbours and society, to be prophets and teachers admired and respected of all men. All these are laudable qualities; no one would wish to blame them or to stop them; but all of them can easily be carried too far. Paul now points out that whatever excellence in any of these directions man may attain, whatever progress he may apparently make, all is valueless without the sweetening and refining power of this Divine quality—Love.

In praising Love Paul does not fall into the error of criticizing others; he does not even criticize his pupils. He does not suggest that the Corinthians lack the great quality. He suggests only that he himself may have too little of it. All hint of possible fault is put in the first person singular. This is one of the beautiful things in this most comprehensively beautiful and harmonious "Hymn of Heavenly Love".

If I have not Love, even though I should be able to speak in the most perfect human fashion and even in superhuman fashion like the angels of God, I should be a mere empty voice, "but a sound and hollow". All the gifts of prophecy, all the vast range of knowledge regarding the mysteries of Nature, the mystic relation of man to God, "the vision of the world and all the wonders that shall be"—valueless is it all without Love. Faith itself is nought; if I should attain to that height of Faith of which the Lord spoke, and should be able to remove mountains—valueless without Love. Boundless charity, the giving of vast sums to help the afflicted and the starving, even the charity that gives itself, the self-sacrifice which goes to the martyr's fire and is burned as a testimony to the truth—valueless without Love. However admirable and splendid it is as a part of one's character, it needs to be completed by Love before it attains to be really good. Love is wholly unselfish; it does not resent injury, it does not envy the good-fortune of another, it does not pride itself on its own excellence, it is humble in estimating itself, it is not provoked or embittered by disappointment. Even if it gains by the wrongdoing of others, it is not made joyful by the advantage it has gained; it rejoices only when the right cause triumphs, whether or not itself is the gainer by the triumph.

Another of the beautiful things in this chapter is that Paul ceases to speak in the first person singular when he mentions the excellence of Love. He will not even suggest that he has himself this quality. He uses the first person when talking of possible faults, but the third person when he mentions excellences. The passage is a perfect pattern of the humility and the unselfishness which it lauds.

Love is the one lasting thing. Everything else, however good it may be, is evanescent. The prophet may lose his power of prophecy, the wise philosopher may cease to be able and great, and his intellect may fail; for these are qualities that are in themselves partial, one-sided, incomplete; they have not attained to the Divine power and perfection. But Love fails not, and is never lost. It is eternal in all its nature, because it is complete and Divine in itself. In our imperfect human nature, when we only see a little darkly and dimly (as in the poor metal mirrors of the ancients), and fail to perceive in the reflected image the real character of the thing itself, we attain to the level of the Divine and the Eternal only in the one thing—true Love.

The last words of this great chapter cannot be expressed in any other way than by quotation. They cannot be explained, because they are so simple and final. They stand there once and for ever, interpreting themselves—to be read and understood by all, but not to be weakened by the feeble attempts of a commentator. "Now abideth Faith, Hope, Love, these three; and the greatest of these is Love."

XXXVI

PAUL'S FAREWELL TO THE HELLENIC CHURCHES

Acts xx. 2-38

PAUL'S third missionary journey ends, like his second, with a visit to Jerusalem; but whereas the earlier visit is dismissed in a few words (XVIII. 21, 22), this later visit is described at great length and in much detail. This indicates that Luke regarded it as a critical and highly important event in history, and it was so for two reasons; first on account of its consequences, viz. Paul's imprisonment (which like that of Jesus was caused by the Jews and carried into effect by Roman soldiers), and his trial in its several stages at Jerusalem, Cæsarea and Rome; and, secondly, on account of his intention to make the visit the conclusion and consummation of a period in his evangelistic work.

The mind of Paul was now full of a great idea. He was to leave the Hellenic lands and the Ægean shores, and go right away into the Latin-speaking West, to Rome and to Spain, and make those regions the sphere of his future work. The end of his letter to the Romans (especially xiv. 21), written during the latter days of his residence in Greece, throws much light on these plans and on this part of Luke's history. Before going to Italy and the West, Paul's work in the Hellenic countries should be completed by bringing the Churches of the four provinces, Galatia, Asia, Macedonia and Achaia, into closer relations with the original Church at Jerusalem, and the feeling of brotherhood and unity should be quickened by the influence of charity. For months, and even years, those Churches had been gathering funds under his directions through weekly contributions; and now, as the final act, delegates from the provinces accompanied Paul, to carry help in money to Jerusalem and to make acquaintance with their Jewish fellow-Christians there.

The Church in Jerusalem was poor, and it was in a position where great service to the Christian cause could be accomplished by the use of money. At the great feasts Jerusalem was crowded with pilgrims, both Jews and Jewish Christians, and there was opportunity for beneficent action and hospitality on those occasions. The pilgrims were often poor: fatigue must have fostered diseases in the crowded city; food was dear when demand was great and supply limited. Generous charity on the part of the Church in Jerusalem was not merely right and Christian, it was also wise and prudent, for it was effective in spreading the knowledge of the truth and in conciliating the good-will of the Jewish strangers who found help and kindness from the Church in their need. Now this was a work in which money could be most effectively employed; and Paul's plan opens up a great historic view of the circumstances and possibilities involved. Such a plan shows true statesmanship and constructive genius, building up the fabric of a great united Church, whose head should be in Jerusalem, while its members were scattered over the whole Roman Empire.

For this purpose Galatia sent as delegates Gaius (Derbe) and Timothy (Lystra); Asia sent Tychicus and Trophimus (probably both of Ephesus); Macedonia sent Sopater (Beroea), Aristarchus and Secundus (Thessalonica), and Luke himself (Philippi). Achaia alone sent no delegate; but possibly it requested Paul to act as its representative, for its contribution in money was liberal.[1]

The party gathered in Troas on the Asiatic coast. It might have been expected that the visit would be timed for the Passover; and probably this was the original intention, but as Paul was on the

[1] The text of xx. 4 is incorrect. The meaning may be got by omitting the words "as far as Asia".

point of sailing from Corinth for Syria, it was discovered that the Jews had a plot to kill him; opportunity for murder would be easily found in a ship crowded with pigrims. He therefore changed his plans, and fixed Pentecost for the visit to Jerusalem, while he himself went to Macedonia and celebrated the Passover at Philippi.

The morning after the days of unleavened bread, Friday, April 15, A.D. 57, Paul with Luke started from Philippi, took ship at Neapolis, reached Troas on Tuesday following, and stayed there seven days, i.e. Tuesday April 19 to Monday 25. On Sunday evening the whole congregation met for the Agape feast with the breaking of bread, and religious services and discourse were prolonged first until midnight and then till daybreak. At midnight the meeting was interrupted by the fall of sleepy Eutychus from the window. Luke, a physician, believed him to be dead; but Paul cheered the company by announcing that Eutychus's life was still in him: the spirit had not yet left the body, and Luke's view evidently is that the spirit was detained in its flight and life thus continued through the power of Paul. Early the next morning, i.e. Monday, the company started from Troas This allotment of the days proceeds according to the ancient rule of counting any part of a day as one day

The ship on which the whole of Paul's company

took passage did not intend to put in at Ephesus, which lay some miles up a narrow river and was difficult of access for passing vessels; but it touched at many other points on the coast from Assos onwards, and it lay at Miletus for several days taking or unloading cargo. Paul used the delay to send for the presbyters of Ephesus, the officials who discharged the duty of bishops or overseers in matters affecting the business and common interests of the congregation; and when they arrived he made an address to them, which Luke reports fully with graphic touches, showing that he was an auditor and eye-witness of the scene.

This address is selected by Luke for report because it marked the end of a period, of which the sermon at Pisidian Antioch formed the beginning. Paul indicates its character as valedictory very clearly. It begins as an address specially to the Ephesians; but as all the delegates from the four provinces were present the speaker passed into a general address to them all (v. 25). Such a change is naturally made by a speaker, and its occurrence in a written report proves that a real spoken address was heard by Luke. Paul soon returned again to the narrower address; a speaker marks easily such transitions by tone and emphasis, but they are more difficult to catch in a written report.

In accordance with its valedictory character, the speech gives a review of Paul's conduct during the three years (so reckoned after the ancient fashion of counting part of the third year as a whole year) which he spent in Ephesus; and all that he says about his action might be applied to his residence in his other Churches throughout the four provinces.

In all he had shown the same humility: in all he had faced the dangers of Jewish enmity: in all he had taught fearlessly the truth. Now he was leaving them, and they among whom he had preached should see his face no longer. The Spirit constrained him to visit Jerusalem; and yet the same Spirit announced to him in every city that imprisonment and affliction awaited him; but life was cheap to him in comparison with the unbroken continuance of his work. In his life among them he had so borne himself that he was blameless whosoever might perish; he had declared the whole truth how they might save themselves. When he declares that he has never used his opportunities as a leader to take the goods of others, such a disclaimer may seem to us rather below the dignity of the address, but Paul was speaking to Orientals, who are rarely scrupulous about turning office into a means of unfair gain; and he was thus politely giving the presbyters advice against a temptation which might assail them in their official life. The standard of action to which those presbyters had been accustomed in their heathen life was very low; and there was always the danger of a relapse into their earlier ways. Paul had maintained himself and his friends by his own labour, in order to set an example of work; and as he spoke of his handiwork, he held up "these hands" to his auditors. He concluded by admonishing them, as overseers, to help the weak and to remember how the Lord Jesus had said: "It is more blessed to give than to receive". This saying does not occur in any of the Gospels; but it is a brief statement of the purport of many passages in the Teaching of Jesus. The advice to help the weak is specially characteristic of Paul's sympathetic nature. To support the weak is among the prime duties both of officials in the Church and of every Christian (1 Thess. v. 14).[1]

[1] See Section XXXII.

XXXVII

THE PROPHETS WHO STOPPED PAUL

Acts xxi. 1-17

THE minute detail of the voyages to Jerusalem and to Italy is remarkable, when we consider how careful Luke is to mention only what was important for his purpose as historian of the growth of the Church through the power of the Spirit. He dwells on them in order to emphasize the importance of the crisis which was connected with them. In a similar fashion in Acts xvi. he dwells on the details of Paul's journey from Lystra to Philippi, in order to bring out in strong relief the power of the Spirit in leading Paul to Macedonia and to Europe.

But beyond this we must recognize something of the personal character of the historian; he had the love of the true Hellene for the sea, and he dwells with interest on details of sea-faring, how Cyprus rose out of the sea on the left, how they passed Mitylene and Cos and many another famous place, how the winds drove them about, and how they had to haul a little boat on board. He had seen these events, and he gives bulk to the important part of the story by recording what specially interested him.

A coasting vessel, which touched at many points, carried the party as far as Patara in Lycia. There they took passage on a larger vessel, which was fitted for the long voyage across the Levant direct to the Syrian coast at Tyre, where they waited seven days while the ship was discharging cargo; and they spent the time in intercourse with the Tyrian congregation.

Here occurred a typical incident. Luke has as yet mentioned only indirectly that in every city the Spirit inspired men to prophesy what awaited Paul in Jerusalem. In Tyre the disciples "said to Paul through the Spirit that he should not set foot in Jerusalem". This revelation was, apparently, couched in the form of an order, prohibiting the journey. Luke gives in this a practical example of the difficulties which may occur, when congregations are to a large extent guided by inspiration granted from time to time by the Spirit. Not every person who is apparently inspired is free from misleading excitement, and not every person who is, in a sense, really inspired, comprehends fully the message that has been entrusted to him to deliver. It is always necessary to examine the messages of apparent inspiration before we accept them, even while we carefully refrain from chilling the enthusiasm of others by unbelief or coldness or ridicule. This is Paul's advice in 1 Thess. v. 21.[1] Such then is the situation set before us in the congregation at Tyre The disciples in that Church, under a real inspiration as to what would happen in the circumstances about which all were anxiously thinking, forbade Paul to go to Jerusalem. Paul knew, however, that such was not the intention of the message. The Spirit was not forbidding him, but merely testing him. It was needful that he should understand well what awaited him : it was needful for the success of his work that all the Churches of the Roman world should realize clearly what dangers he was facing while he followed the path of duty. Hence these repeated warnings. In Tyre the warning was mistaken by the disciples for a prohibition, but Paul was not misled. For us it is important to observe how Luke's history sets before us in practical form the situations and the difficulties with which Paul deals in his letters. The Acts cannot be thoroughly understood apart from the Epistles, and should not be read without constant reference to them.

[1] Also 1 John iv. 1 see Section XXXII

When the ship was ready to sail on the seventh day, the entire congregation, men, women and children, accompanied Paul and his friends to the sea-shore; and they separated with prayer. So ends this passing glimpse which is given us of the Tyrian Church, one of the many which had come into existence unrecorded along that coast. This chance visit, and the enforced delay caused by trading arrangements, have preserved the picture. The words which Luke uses, "when it came to pass that we had accomplished the days," suggest that the delay was a little irksome, in spite of the kindly and gracious intercourse with the little body of Tyrian Christians, who had to be sought out in that great city. But Paul was eager to reach Cæsarea, from whence the land-road to Jerusalem began He knew Cæsarea from of old; and he evidently looked forward to meeting Philip there once more. There was natural sympathy between the Apostle of the Gentiles and the man who had first broken the ties of race and sect, and had frankly preached to the despised Samaritans.

In Cæsarea the company remained a number of days, for the voyage had been so successful that Pentecost was not yet arrived. They went direct to Philip's house, and the time which they still had free was spent in intercourse with him and the four prophetesses his daughters.

Our view is that this intercourse had great influence on the composition of Luke's history, and that Philip was one of the authorities on whom the historian most relied for the events narrated in the first part of the book. Luke does not attribute the delay here to external causes, as he does at Tyre. They willingly spent the days in the enjoyment of Philip's hospitality, until the time when they must start for Jerusalem. During this interval Agabus, the same prophet who had foretold in Antioch the great famine, arrived from Jerusalem; and with the symbolic action of an old Hebrew prophet he showed how the Jews at Jerusalem would bind Paul and deliver him into the hands of the Gentiles.

It is noteworthy with what insistence Luke dwells on these successive warnings which Paul heard and disregarded. A great and justly respected modern scholar has pointed out that the prophecy of Agabus was not fulfilled, and has made this the ground for a charge of carelessness and inaccuracy against Luke. But it was not Luke's purpose to make Agabus literally exact; his purpose was to tell what occurred as it occurred. The prophecy was in a general, though not in a literal, way fulfilled; and the incident brings out in strong relief Paul's firm resolution and his tenderness of heart. Even the weeping entreaties of his dearest friends could not break his resolve, though they might break his heart. Perhaps, also, Luke is here again illustrating the necessity of extreme caution in understanding the prophetic messages granted to the Church. Even Agabus, whose prediction had been so important in an old crisis of the Church, was in this case only disturbing the Will of God and the great plan of Paul, and he was only ideally, but not literally, accurate in his prediction. Prophecies might fail (1 Cor. XIII. 10), but Love never failed.

The journey to Jerusalem was one of sixty miles, and some preparation and equipment were required (v. 15). The disciples in Cæsarea aided and escorted Paul. Horses were needed to make such a journey in the two days which seem to have been allowed, and the true translation of v. 16 is that the escort conducted Paul to his host for the night, one Mnason, an early disciple. The place for breaking the journey was probably Lydda; and there we must look for Mnason's house. On the morrow the party went on to Jerusalem, where they were welcomed by the brethren. The whole party visited James on the following day, and the interview was interesting and momentous.

We are struck, however, with three facts: (1) Luke does not mention the special purpose of the visit and the presentation of the money, except incidentally in XXIV. 17; (2) he says little about the attitude or the hospitality of the Church in Jerusalem (except the emphatic " gladly " in v. 17); (3) he says nothing about the impression which the first view of Jerusalem made on those travellers, though he does record their first view of Cyprus. One may probably infer that there was a certain lack of sympathy between Luke and those Jewish Christians who had remained in Jerusalem and were rather old-fashioned. A devoted friend of Paul, he was never quite cordial to Jews, who so often were hostile to his hero and teacher.

XXXVIII

THE CHURCH AND ITS ENEMIES IN THE PAGAN WORLD

Review: Acts XIV.-XXI.

DURING Paul's first journey towards the West it would appear probable that he had no definite plan of work. He was driven on, partly by the command of the Holy Spirit, given through the prophets as well as spoken directly to himself, partly by the overmastering desire in his own soul to spread the truth which he had learned These two forces which impelled him were really expressions of the one ultimate fact. The Spirit ordered him to do what he was born to do. He himself was eager to do it, because the impulse and the power were in his heart and dominated his whole nature. As he, in after years, looked back on his past life,[1] he recognized that he was before his birth chosen out by the purpose of God for this work; that all the circumstances of his

[1] See Galatians I. 9 ff

birth, his family, his early training as a child, and his later experiences as a young man, had been such as to fit him for the apostleship of the Gentiles; and that throughout all the maze of his early manhood, his studies in the Jewish Holy Law at Jerusalem, and his fanatical persecution of the early Church, the Will of God had been goading him into the proper path for which he was intended.

That he was conscious of this destiny when he sailed to Cyprus, we cannot doubt: it had been expressly and repeatedly intimated to him by the Spirit. But how and by what methods he was to accomplish his destiny he had to learn in the school of experience. He had to begin with tentatives, he had to try one course and another, even to make mistakes and thereby find guidance.

He soon recognized that Cyprus and Pamphylia were not his field of work. After a time, however, he became conscious that the Galatian churches were the beginning of his Gospel: there first he had definitely turned to the Gentiles. Those Gentiles to whom he felt himself specially suited to speak and called upon to speak, were the people of the Roman Empire, among whom he had been born a citizen, among whom he had acquired his knowledge of Western civilization and methods and thought, to whom he was indebted for much.

Opinion may differ as to how far he was conscious of this definite bent to the Roman world in his first journey; but there can hardly exist a doubt in any mind that he was fully aware of it in the beginning of his second journey. Through Galatia he was then directing his course to the great and highly civilized province of Asia;[1] but his purpose was barred, and he was forbidden to speak there. Only after long and perplexing wanderings did he at last learn that the Spirit was shepherding him into Europe, to the provinces of Macedonia and Achaia.

Yet Asia also must be conquered for the truth, and was the chief work of his third journey. Why this was so, why he had to go first to more distant provinces, and then fill up the intervening gap by subsequent work, we can only conjecture. Perhaps it was in order that he might learn to take wider views, and that his loving interest in his earlier churches might not betray him into confining his attention to them. It is, at any rate, certain that this was one of the lessons which he learned on his second journey, for on his third journey he was looking to Rome and Spain: he was bent on reaching the farthest bounds of the West, and afterwards filling in the intermediate space. There was no longer any fear that he

[1] The province Asia included only the western part of Asia Minor.

might narrow his interest to his early churches. Much as he loved them, he was now resolved to leave them to work out their own destiny with the help of his trusted companions and coadjutors, such as Timothy, and under the guidance of the Spirit, which was always inspiring those congregations. His third journey was his farewell to the East, and the prelude to a wider work in the West, as has been clearly brought out in the last few Sections.

That the progress of the new Faith was marvellously rapid is a fact once doubted by modern scholars, but now almost universally admitted; only those who ignore historical evidence can doubt it. What were the causes that contributed to this? We may assume here what has been already said in the previous reviews,[1] especially as to the power and guidance of the Spirit: all that was there said applies equally here.

The great fact in the pagan world at this epoch was that the fullness of time was come. The world was in need, and was conscious of the need, of a Divine Saviour. People had gradually been driven by bitter experience to the conclusion that society was sick unto death, and could not be cured by human means. The attempts of philosophy to furnish a cure might satisfy a few exceptional

[1] Chaps. XIII. and XXV.

minds, but could not touch the popular heart. The common man everywhere was looking for Divine aid, and had neither confidence in, nor hope of, any other help. The doctrine of a Saviour, God manifesting himself in human form to cure the evils of society, appealed to the heart of the pagan world: that was what men generally believed to be necessary, and what they were looking for.

The enemies in the pagan world which the new Faith had to contend against were many, but three are conspicuous:—

1. The paganism that ruled in the Eastern provinces was a very degraded form of religion, which had almost entirely lost the germs of true insight into Divine nature and goodness that once existed in it. It ministered to and encouraged all the vices of society. It had become an unmixed evil; and there was nothing to be done with it except to eradicate it. The more educated classes of pagan society had risen superior to it, and had no belief in it, though they had nothing better to put in its place. Idolatry therefore was to Paul the great enemy: it meant darkness, degradation, infamy, and degeneration for mankind. He desired to make men virtuous, chaste, innocent, truthful. Paganism and the service of idols not merely failed to inculcate those goods, but actually patronized and encouraged the opposite vices, unchastity,

drunkenness, untruthfulness. The only redeeming fact about the established paganism was its weakness : men set small store by it; the very priests did not believe in it.

2. Magic and witchcraft often replaced the belief in paganism. The gods were powerless, and were recognized to be powerless; and the Christian teachers were often opposed by sorcerers, who made money out of their dupes. The events which occurred at Philippi, Samaria, Paphos and Ephesus, exemplify the nature of this enemy, and need not be again recounted But it is noteworthy that the magicians were not such hateful enemies as the common idolatry was: they possessed some knowledge, perverted and dangerous indeed, but still a sort of knowledge; and they could recognize the truth after a fashion.

3. The supreme enemy was the Roman State and its religion, which consisted in the worship of the living emperor as the embodiment in human form of a Divine idea, and of the deceased emperors as deified in heaven. Paul's attitude to this enemy was mixed. On the one hand, as being idolatrous in character, it was hateful and abominable. But on the other hand, as being the power of good law, of order, and of peace, it was in a certain way the friend of the new Faith. It permitted the Christians to teach. It protected them against illegal and

riotous attacks, especially on the part of the Jews. Many of its officials were friendly to Paul. It had a certain part to play for a time in the spread of the Faith; but ultimately it must be destroyed and give place to the kingdom of Christ. Meanwhile, it must be obeyed until it was altered.

XXXIX

FREEDOM IN EVERYDAY LIFE

1 *Cor*. x. 23-33

The Corinthian Church, which consisted mainly of Greeks (with a few Romans and a few Jews), had the Greek characteristic of a love for argument and theory and endless discussion. They had caught up a phrase, which Paul himself had used, " all things are lawful for me," and quoted it, apart from the qualifying and limiting context, in support of arguments which Paul could not accept (vi. 12, x. 23). Paul had been speaking in favour of Christian freedom: that which is not in itself wrong is lawful. So far, that is quite true; but it needs much qualification in practical life. An action may be quite lawful, but very inadvisable. A person who is trying to break himself of the smoking habit would not be wise to travel in a smoking carriage. A reformed drunkard, anxious to do right, but still weak, should not pass through the street where his old cronies are wont to assemble. As a general rule, unless an action tends in itself to cause positive good, one may well think twice about doing it.

But further, in all one's life and actions it is right to think about the effect that may be produced on one's neighbours and associates, and not simply to consider whether it is lawful or expedient or convenient for oneself. The Christian congregation is a band of brethren; and the interests of the whole brotherhood should be considered in all that one does. A life which is led on the principle of doing all that is lawful for oneself is a purely selfish life, and is therefore not a Christian life.

This general rule Paul now applies to a question which was much discussed in the early Church, and which presented itself in practice constantly to every Christian. Society was at that time organized on a pagan basis. The forms and ceremonies of ordinary courtesy in private society and in political and commercial life were pagan in character. Public meetings were opened with pagan ceremonial: ought a Christian therefore to refrain from using his rights and performing his duties as a citizen? The giving thanks to God before and after meat took a pagan form, as an "invocation of the gods". Was a Christian to absent himself from every social meeting in a pagan house, and confine himself absolutely to the society of Christians? To do so would cut him off from many opportunities of benefiting his fellow-citizens and of spreading the knowledge of the truth, and would amount almost to a "boycott" of all non-Christians by the Christians. How far was it justifiable or right to accept the established forms of social intercourse, and to ignore the pagan character in many of those forms?

This was always a difficult question, and it was answered in varying fashion by different persons and in different circles. Some were far more strict in this matter than others. The question answered itself in later times, when Christians became the majority, and the forms of social courtesy took a Christian character. But in the first century it was a burning question. It presented itself in a very acute form in regard to the eating of meats that had been offered to idols. Much of the flesh sold in the butchers' shops was cut from victims that had been offered in sacrifice. Many of the dinner parties given in society followed after a religious ceremony, such as a marriage or the coming of age of a son; and the flesh set on the table was that of the animals which had been offered in sacrifice to the gods. When a Christian bought meat in a shop, was he to ask whether it was sacrificial? Paul answers unhesitatingly:

No. The earth is the Lord's, and everything that is in the earth has been made by Him, and all that He made is good. The ox is good in itself: the idol to which it has been offered is a thing of nought: the flesh of the animal remains the same, whether offered or not offered: the idol has no effect upon it.

Again, if a Christian was invited to a dinner-party by a pagan friend in his own house, and accepted the invitation, was he to ask, as each dish was set on the table, whether it had been offered in sacrifice? Here, again, Paul unhesitatingly answers: No. Eat whatsoever is set before you, asking no rude question: courtesy requires this, and Christian principle does not forbid it. Social intercourse would be impossible, and all the amenities and grace of life would be destroyed, if such questions were obtruded on the company in which one had taken one's place. It is open to any one to refrain from going into the society of those who differ in religious opinions; but "if ye are disposed to go" into their society, then the customs of polished courtesy should be observed.

One exception, however, is made by the Apostle. If some one should challenge you and pointedly declare that the meat set before you has been offered to an idol, then you should not eat of it— you should refrain, not for your sake and because of your conscience, but for his sake. He is probably a person of delicate and over-scrupulous conscience; and he may have doubts as to whether it is right to eat such food, and yet seeing you eat he may through shame-facedness be induced to do what he believes to be wrong and eat like you. Thus your freedom may be a snare to your brother. This is a principle of conduct, to which one must always have regard in one's daily life: one must think not merely of one's own feelings and judgment about right and wrong, but also about the effect which one's actions may have upon fellow-Christians. There are actions from which one should refrain, even though one sees nothing wrong in them, simply because they may give offence or cause danger and error to one's brethren in the congregation. A Christian must always sympathize with and be mindful of his brother-Christians and act for their sake as well as for his own.

Yet while one sympathizes with the weaker and more delicate conscience of others, and refrains from hurting or misleading them, one must preserve one's own freedom and strength of mind. One should in those cases refrain consciously for the sake of others, and not lose one's own boldness and freedom. We should not suffer their conscience to be the judge of our liberty. In such matters the robust conscience is the healthy one: the delicate conscience, which is always on its guard, and is constantly in terror of doing anything wrong, is weak. But one must have regard to one's weaker brother, and not allow one's own freedom to do him harm; though one feels that the true Christian is strong, bold and decided, not weak, apprehensive of evil, and timorous. Above all, one should refuse to allow the weak to condemn the strong. "If I partake with thankfulness of such meat, then I should not be condemned or evil spoken of regarding the food for which I thanked God" It may happen that we hear some weaker Christians tell with horror and condemnation that such another dined with a pagan and ate meat of an animal that had been slain in sacrifice to Jupiter or some other idol. In such a case we should not keep silence and allow him to be condemned: we should defend him and take his part. The main rule of conduct for Christians should always be, even in such small matters as eating or drinking, to consider whether the act will conduce to the glory of God and the enlargement of His kingdom. In His kingdom there are both Jews who are over-scrupulous about small rules of life, and Greeks who are freer in mind. Let us refrain from offending either Jews by needlessly outraging their scruples, or Greeks by trying to impose on them the narrower rules of Jewish scrupulousness.

After writing this paragraph Paul seems to have felt that something was needed to complete it. We are conscious, as we read it, that in pleading for liberty he has expressed himself in terms which are a little hard in tone. There is an element which must be added to modify and to perfect this tenth chapter; and through consciousness of this Paul adds in Chapter XIII. the wonderful exposition of the power of Christian love and the urgent importance of bringing love to bear on all matters of life and conduct, which forms the subject of Section XXXV.

XL

SELF-DENIAL THE PROOF OF LOVE

Rom. xiv. 10-21

THE subject treated in the previous Section was one which could not be exhausted in a brief space. Paul returned to it on other occasions, and especially in a paragraph of his letter to the Romans. How should the Christian live in the pagan world? The question is always hard to answer; but it was specially hard for the earliest Churches. The situation was new. No system of Christian teaching about the manifold difficulties of practical life amid an alien society had been formed. The questions which arose were often complicated; and it was easy for even a trusted and wise adviser to misunderstand the full import of each problem as it came before him, and to lose sight of some of the many issues that were involved. Mistakes were certainly made by persons whose intentions were good; and wide differences of opinion about the same questions existed within the Church.

The early Christians, small groups scattered over the ancient cities in the midst of a numerous pagan society, had to decide what their conduct should be in many delicate matters of social conduct and etiquette. Political meetings for voting or for judicial or other purposes always began with some pagan religious ceremony. Was the Christian citizen to abandon his right of voting, to give up all share in political life, and to absent himself from all public meetings, or should he attend them and take a part, though only a silent part, in a pagan ceremony? All magistrates of each city had to take an official position in the many religious rites which were performed to ensure for the State or the city the favour of the gods. Were Christians to refrain from the career of public service, or could they take official part in those rites?

In private life similar difficulties faced them. If they went to a social gathering, or a dinner party, there were pagan sacred rites to sanctify the assembly. The saying of grace before eating and after took the form of a rite in honour of a false god. Yet the acknowledgment of the Divine kindness and grace, which was made by pagans at every meal, was in itself a right thing, which every Christian must approve and regard as springing from a true instinct, though misdirected. If one bought a piece of meat in a butcher's shop, it was usually (as has been mentioned in Section XXXIX) the flesh of a victim that had been offered in sacrifice at some pagan temple.

Thus the life of a tiny group of Christians in a pagan city was compassed about with a cloud of difficulties. If a member of the little congregation was to make it his first object to avoid all participation in idolatry and all contact with anything that had idolatrous associations, his daily life would be spent and wasted in investigating a multitude of details, since he was at every step brought into some kind of relation with something idolatrous; and he would have no time or energy left for the greater things of life. He could only with difficulty get out of the presence of an idol, for idols were everywhere in the streets and in the houses, painted on the walls, or cut in stone or wood, or moulded of clay or metal.

Would it be wise, or even permissible and justifiable, to inquire scrupulously into the history of every article sold in an ordinary shop, lest it might have come in contact with an idol? That would practically mean that the Christian "must needs go out of the world," as Paul remarks in 1 Cor. v. 9; for there was no room left for them in their native cities. Ought the Christians to cut themselves off wholly from social intercourse with their pagan neighbours? If they did so, they would lose many opportunities of coming into relations with them and influencing them. If the Christian were to criticize and blame every idolatrous action of his pagan neighbours which came before his eyes, he would make life unendurable for himself and for his neighbours.

The fact remained inevitable that the Christian in a pagan city must shut his eyes to, and tacitly acquiesce in, much that was idolatrous, and much that he disapproved and hated. The difficult question was to determine when he ought to cease to acquiesce and begin to show open disapproval. The question was answered differently by different persons. Some engaged in the public service, as officials or magistrates or soldiers, and allowed the inevitable pagan rites to be performed in their presence. Some avoided public service as far as possible, showing themselves far more scrupulous and tender of conscience ; and these were blamed by their pagan neighbours as unpatriotic, morose, and idle, because they left the duties of public life to others who were more willing to work for the public good.

Innumerable such questions faced every Christian daily. He must answer them in his life, and the answers given were necessarily various. From this variety of conduct sprang another difficulty. Those who were scrupulous were apt to condemn those who allowed themselves greater latitude, while the free-minded were apt to condemn as weak-minded those who showed themselves more scrupulous. It was an almost greater difficulty that some people, who felt it wrong to act with bold freedom in their intercourse with society and in political life, were yet so much coerced by fear of contempt or ridicule from their strong-minded brethren that they used a freedom which they felt to be wrong, and thus endangered their character and conscience.

Paul has now to lay down general principles of conduct, which may guide his congregations in these minor points of life, and his first rule is that Christians shall be slow to judge one another. Neither should the scrupulous man condemn his brother for being too free, nor the bolder man condemn his brother for being weak and over-scrupulous. We must all be judged by God; we are all God's servants; we have therefore no right to occupy God's place as judge of His servants. One judgment alone we must rigorously pass upon ourselves, that we do nothing which may hinder the moral development of any of our fellow-Christians. It must of course be remembered that Paul is not here speaking about the great questions of moral right and wrong. There are cases where a brother falls into real wrongdoing and crime;

and then it becomes our duty to condemn and even, in extreme cases, to hold aloof from the evildoer. Paul is here concerned with matters about which opinion may reasonably and justly differ.

The right line of conduct will be determined by love. You may feel that a meat is not made unclean because the animal was sacrificed to a pagan god; but do not wound a brother's feelings while you display your freedom of mind by eating it. Christ died to save him: will you not deny yourself in this small matter to help him? Will you put a strain on his conscience, and perhaps lead him into doing what he thinks wrong? Any matter of food and drink belongs in itself to mere human life, and is not a part of the kingdom of God; such matters are temporary, evanescent, and unreal. We should live in and for the kingdom of God, i.e. for what is eternal, enduring, and true; and to that category belong righteousness, peace, and joy in the Spirit, not meats and drink. These greater things we shall attain by seeking always to do what will tend to produce peace among our brethren, and to build them up in goodness of character. In itself wine, like meat, is not evil; but it is evil in its effect on the character and life of society. Do not for the sake of a mere drink overthrow the work of God; for that is what you do if you help by your example to spread the habit of intoxication. You will show the true spirit of love in your action, you will foster throughout the whole sphere of society in which you are placed the mighty realities of goodness, concord, and joy in the Holy Spirit, if you sacrifice even your free-mindedness in order to avoid wounding the feelings or endangering the moral improvement of your neighbours and brothers.

Hold your own beliefs as far as you can justify them to God, but let your beliefs be between God and yourself. In your action and life think of your neighbour, and show your love for him. It is not your beliefs, but your conduct and your love and your self-sacrifice, that make your life These are the things that stand the test, and last through time into the eternal kingdom of God.

Thus those difficult questions of conduct which the early Christians had to answer in their life, and many delicate questions which we in the modern world must answer one way or another in our action, are best solved, not by abstract discussions as to what is right or wrong, justifiable or unjustifiable; but by applying the practical test, which course of action helps our brother, tends to improve society, and to establish righteousness and peace and joy in the world.

In this treatment of the question, addressed to the Romans, one feels the influence of that wonderful chapter about love, 1 Cor. XIII. The tone in which the question is treated seems gentler here than in 1 Cor. x. (see previous Section); and yet the answer is not essentially different; only the tone is changed. To the Romans Paul insists less on freedom, and more on love. Freedom is a noble thing; but love for one's brother is nobler. The Apostle's view is practically the same in both passages; but in the first he lays more stress on the Christian right to be free, in the second he speaks far more of the Christian duty to act with love and sympathy. In this life of ours it is usually far more needful to strengthen our love for our neighbour than our desire for freedom to do as we think right. We are all very keenly alive to our rights; but we are not always so vividly conscious of our duties.

XLI

THE BEGINNING OF THE CRISIS

Acts XXI. 17–XXII. 29

AFTER the informal welcome on the day of their arrival, the delegates were formally received on the following day by James and all the elders of the Jerusalem congregation. Luke was present. He does not intimate that he was present at any of the subsequent proceedings in Jerusalem or Cæsarea, but when the voyage to Rome was beginning he resumes the use of the first person plural. During the intervening period he must have been near Paul; but he was not actually taking part in any of the incidents that occurred, and hence he could not with propriety employ the first person. This is evident to anyone who reads the intervening chapters and contrasts them with the paragraphs where the narrative is expressed in the first person plural.

Paul conveyed the salutations of the Gentile Churches, and narrated the story of their growth and all that they had done. The elders made suitable

XLI. THE BEGINNING OF THE CRISIS

acknowledgment, and then turned to the topic which was weighing on all minds, viz. Paul's danger.

To guard against this was a prime necessity. The elders pointed out that there was great misapprehension even among the Jewish Christians as to what Paul had done and taught among the Gentiles. He had changed the front of the Christian Church; he had made it look towards the Gentile world, and he was himself looking towards Rome and Spain for its future growth, rather than towards Palestine. Even the Christian Jews were suspicious of the change, and there were many thousands of them (chaps. IV. 4, VI. 1, VIII. 1, IX. 32, etc.). Their suspicions were fed by false reports spread in Jerusalem by the Jews from Asia and the other provinces, when they came up to the great Feasts in Jerusalem. These declared that Paul was teaching the Jews to abandon all the customs of their forefathers and the Law of Moses; and such reiterated reports (the Greek verb in XXI. 21 is far stronger than the English "informed") had produced a strong prejudice against Paul among even Christian Jews, while the non-Christian Jews were enraged in the highest degree. When great numbers of Jews, Christian and non-Christian, were collected in Jerusalem for Pentecost, the situation was very grave.

James and the elders, in this passage of the Acts, are the same persons who are called in the Epistle to the Hebrews XIII. 24 " them that have the rule over you ". It is clear that in that Epistle the persons addressed are the mass of the Palestinian Christians, who were not in perfect agreement with their rulers regarding Paul's teaching and conduct, and who looked on the Apostle of the Gentiles with suspicion and even dislike. Luke here implies exactly that situation. James and the elders, who were " the rulers," are evidently anxious that Paul should now disabuse the minds of the Jewish Christians of their misapprehension and suspicion regarding his action and his principles.

Luke does not inform us why the elders had apparently made no attempt to explain Paul's real attitude to the mass of the Christian Jews: certainly they speak here as if the prejudice had spread uncontradicted, and it looks as if Luke were thus indicating that the elders had not been sufficiently careful of Paul's interests. He does not blame them, but he refrains from praising them. Now, however, they showed themselves anxious to avert the danger. Probably the coming of the delegates and the full statement of the actual facts had dissipated some prejudice from their minds. Paul's intention in this embassy from the new Churches to the old seemed to be in process of fulfilment.

XLI. THE BEGINNING OF THE CRISIS

The suggestion was made that Paul should display to the multitude his personal observance of the Law. There were four men known to the elders as having taken a vow: these had to pay their vow by sacrificing and by shaving the beard and dedicating the hair that had grown during the month preceding. The expenses of the ceremony were considerable, and rich Jews often showed charity by paying the charges incurred by poor men in this way. It was proposed that Paul should pay the charges for these four men, and should perform the ceremonies along with them in the temple; and he immediately proceeded to act upon the suggestion. The ceremonial lasted in regular course through seven days.

About the fifth or sixth day the storm burst. Some Asian Jews saw Paul in the holy part of the temple, where no Gentiles might intrude on pain of death. These Jews knew that he had been accompanied by two Asian Gentiles; and immediately, without any investigation, they inferred (or pretended to believe) that he had brought his travelling companions with him into the temple. They seized Paul and shouted for help, explaining loudly their charge against him. All the Jews rushed on Paul and dragged him out of the temple, and the officials closed the doors (which ordinarily should have stood open) against the hated and impious criminal. When Paul was about to be murdered by his assailants, the Tribune who commanded the Roman garrison in the tower of Antonia (which dominated the temple and with it the city), hearing of the riot, ran hastily down the stairs that led from the tower to the temple with a troop of soldiers and their officers, and saved Paul from the hands of the Jews, but bound him with two chains. The officer then tried to learn what was the cause of the riot; but the confusion was too great, so he ordered Paul to be brought up into the castle.

Such was the crowd and its violence that Paul had to be carried by the soldiers up the stairs; but when he was at the entrance to the castle, he seized an opportunity of explaining to the Tribune that he was not a rebel, but a Jew and a citizen of that important city Tarsus. The fact that, at this moment, when he was bruised and doubtless bleeding from the violence and blows of the Jews, and excited with the struggle and the rescue from imminent death, he should have spoken of Tarsus with such pride, shows that the memory of his own city, the home of his childhood, lay always close to his heart.

Further, Paul's every word and act at this moment of supreme danger evince remarkable courage, coolness and self-possession. His one thought now was to seize the occasion of speaking to the people, when he had a great crowd before him with their attention fixed on him. This might be an opportunity of bringing home the truth to them; and, with the Tribune's permission, standing on the stairs, he beckoned to the people and addressed them in the national tongue, Aramaic. The use of the Semitic speech instead of Greek (which probably the whole audience understood, and the foreign Jews generally knew better than the Jewish vernacular) marked in itself his claim to be a true Hebrew. Paul was a good linguist: he could evidently speak with equal ease and power in Greek and Aramaic: he knew the ancient Hebrew of the Bible; and when he planned to visit Spain he must have been confident that he could address the audiences of the cities there in Latin.

The speech which he made on the castle stairs was a defence against the charges which (as he knew) were being privately made against him, of having forsaken his nation and abjured the Mosaic law and profaned the temple. His plan was to bring home to the people the real facts by a sketch of his life, showing how bigoted a Hebrew he had been from childhood, how true he had been to the Jewish tradition and custom, how bitterly he had persecuted the Christians, how finally he had been convinced of his error only by the direct intervention and orders of God himself.

His account of his persecuting "unto the death" does not imply that he had intentionally been instrumental in putting to death other Christians than Stephen alone. The words do not necessarily indicate more than the death of one Christian: and the Jews had not the authority to execute. only some isolated sudden outbreak of fanaticism and murder under great provocation might be (and usually was) allowed by the Roman government to pass unpunished, but such conduct could not be permitted to be carried on systematically.

For example, in the present case, if the Tribune had been too late in intervening, and if he had found Paul already dead or at the point of death, probably no notice would have been taken of the crime, because the explanation would have been accepted that Paul was detected in the act of bringing foreigners into the forbidden place, and that the passion of the mob was roused to frenzy. But the Tribune succeeded by his quickness in preventing the crime; and so it might have been in the case of Stephen, if there had been a sufficiently active and watchful Roman officer at hand, eager to stop riots at the beginning.

It is to be observed how much stress Paul lays on the superhuman element in his conversion. In this supreme moment, barely rescued from death, he spoke from the depths of his heart the truth as he knew it. He was profoundly convinced that God had repeatedly revealed His Will directly to His servant. It was, however, vain to hope that the passionate excitement of the mob could be calmed by an appeal to facts; and the moment that he named the Gentiles, the word recalled the crime of which his assailants believed him to be guilty, and their frenzy broke out anew.

Paul was then taken into the castle, and the Tribune proposed to examine him by torture as a barbarian and a criminal, who would speak the truth only under the lash, but Paul appealed to his rights as a Roman, and proceedings were instantly stopped and changed.

XLII

THE REAL ISSUE BETWEEN PAUL AND THE JEWS

Acts XXII. 30–XXIII. 35

ALTHOUGH Paul was now safe for the moment, his position was still a dangerous one. The first duty of every Roman Governor was to maintain peace; if he failed to do that, he was responsible. Now Paul was a source of disorder; he stood alone against a nation; but the nation would be pacified if the one man were slain; and in such a situation few Roman officers would hesitate to take the easy way of securing quiet, without investigating too carefully the rights of the case. The Tribune had been on the point of torturing Paul to extort a confession, after which the prisoner would have been executed and peace restored. Paul was saved by the influence and privilege which belonged to him as a Roman. Yet even against a Roman the charge of having, however unintentionally, caused a riot was grave; and, for the governor of such a troublesome populace as the Jews, there was always a strong temptation to propitiate them by sacrificing the hated individual. One man would die and the nation would be saved. The analogy of Paul's case to the seizure and execution of the Saviour must have been present to Luke's mind in this part of his narrative.

A preliminary investigation was held on the following day by the Tribune in order to determine the real facts, which as yet he had been unable to discover; and he called the supreme national Council to help him in the investigation. The meeting thus convoked by a Roman military officer was not a formal assembly presided over by the high-priest in his official dress; it was an informal meeting of the councillors aiding the Tribune to determine the facts. Neither the Council nor the Tribune had the right to condemn a Roman; but, if there seemed to be a case against him, a proper report of the facts must be made to the Governor of the province, who was styled Procurator. At this meeting Luke could hardly have been present, and his knowledge was probably derived from Paul himself.

The account of the meeting is incomplete; it was doubtless opened by a statement from the Tribune as to why he had called the assembly, and what he had done; but Luke hurries on to the point where Paul was called to speak for himself. The prisoner began with the remarkable words, addressed not to the Tribune, but to the councillors of his nation, "Brethren, I have acted as a citizen in all good conscience before God unto this day". The sequel shows that these words were in some way peculiarly offensive to the Jews; and as we do not know what had been said previously, we can only guess what was the cause. There is no reason to think that the Jews would be offended because they considered that the prisoner was speaking in a self-righteous tone, for the words are only a protest in Jewish style that he was innocent and faithful to the religion of the nation. But the single word " acted-as-a-citizen " seemed to the Jews of Palestine to amount almost to an unconscious confession of guilt. The accusation against Paul was that he sacrificed Jewish customs to Greek, and he here used a word which was characteristically Greek, and which assimilated the Jewish life under Divine rule to the godless, free, self-governing life of Greek citizens. The thought and word constituted an insult to the Hebrew spirit, and the high-priest Ananias bade those who were beside Paul smite him on the mouth.

Paul's indignation at such treatment flamed out in the disrespectful passionate words of verse 3. He did not know that it was the high-priest who had spoken, for he had been absent from Jerusalem (except perhaps in xviii. 22) since Ananias was appointed; and the latter was sitting as an ordinary member of the Council with a Roman presiding. His hot retort roused a cry of horror, "answerest thou the high-priest so?" Paul, learning who had spoken, apologized instantly in words quoted from the Greek version of Exodus xxviii. 28 (differing slightly from the Hebrew version).

There followed an incident which has caused much difficulty and great variety of opinion among modern readers. Paul perceived that there was a want of harmony in the Council, some being Sadducees and some Pharisees. We have seen that the attitude of the two factions towards the Jewish Christians was very different, though they were united for the time by common hostility towards Stephen. Paul had always been a Pharisee from personal conviction and through heredity and early training; and he understood the Pharisaic point of view. The temporary union between the two Jewish parties could not obliterate their deep-seated disagreement; and Paul, who always claimed to be still a true Pharisee, a member of the patriot and popular party, opposed to the cold and aristocratic Sadducees, described the nature of the charge against him in a way which would attract to himself the sympathy of the Pharisees Luke saw nothing wrong or unworthy in this, and he was best able to judge. Paul was winning over the Pharisees not merely to himself, but to the Christian cause. He was showing them the real issue that was involved, withdrawing their attention from the secondary issue of his own personal case, and concentrating it on the true nature of Jewish patriotism. He maintained that the true Jewish patriot and the true Pharisee should be a Christian, as he himself was a Pharisee while a Christian (Phil. III. 6): it was only misapprehension of the facts that united Pharisees with Sadducees against the Faith which was bringing Judaism into its proper line of development. Yet Canon Farrar in his "Life of Paul" mourns with deep sorrow over Paul's words, "concerning the hope and resurrection of the dead am I called in question," on the ground that they are a clever trick of misrepresentation and special pleading, suitable for a smart lawyer, but unworthy of the great Apostle. They do not misrepresent the case; they go below the surface, and touch the real nature of the situation. The hope of a Messiah could be fulfilled only through the resurrection of the dead, and the Resurrection of Jesus was the guarantee of the wider hope for all men (1 Cor. xv. 14). Paul states the same view more fully in xxvi. 6-8, where there is no question of a clever trick, for there were no Pharisees among his judges,

XLII. REAL ISSUE BETWEEN PAUL AND JEWS

So keen dissension now arose between the two factions in the Council, that Paul was like to be torn in pieces during their quarrel; and the Tribune took him away to the castle for safety.

In the night that followed Paul was cheered by a vision of the Lord, who stood by him and told him that he must bear witness at Rome. The great plan should be fulfilled: the visit to Jerusalem, which Paul intended as a preliminary to his Roman work (as we have seen), was to be so, though the manner in which he should go to Rome was not that which he had had in mind.

The Divine will was working out Paul's intention after its own fashion; and his life in the following years was not arranged as he had intended, when he spoke to the elders of Ephesus and told them that his work in that region was finished, and they should see his face no more. He went to Rome, but as a prisoner; and he came again to Ephesus and to Macedonia to revisit his churches and to complete his work. Luke is careful to show that at every critical point in his career Paul was guided and informed by direct revelation of God. This is implicated in the structure of Acts; and you cannot get rid of the superhuman element without discarding the whole book.

Next day came a sudden change of scene. Paul's family, which Luke has not previously mentioned, had not wholly deserted him when he became a Christian. His nephew came to reveal a plot against his life ; and the Tribune, recognizing from the nature of the conspiracy and the desperate character of the Jewish fanatics that Paul was not safe in Jerusalem, sent him under a strong guard to Cæsarea, which was reached after a journey on horseback lasting through the night and the following day. The letter which the Tribune wrote to the Procurator misstates the circumstances, because the writer wishes to present his own conduct in the most favourable light, and pretends that his action from the beginning was intended to save a Roman citizen from molestation by Jews. A touch like this shows the truth of real life : the letter contradicts Luke's narrative, but the difference is due to the nature of the Tribune, and proves the excellence of Luke's knowledge and the accuracy of his history.

XLIII

PROGRESS OF PAUL'S CASE IN PALESTINE

Acts XXIV.

THE Jews, finding that the plot against Paul's life had been foiled by the Tribune's sudden action in sending the prisoner to Cæsarea, resolved to follow him thither and prosecute the case before the highest authority in the province.

The Tribune had shifted the responsibility from himself to the Governor, claiming at the same time credit which he hardly deserved for zeal in saving a Roman from the Jewish mob. The officer had been on the whole kindly in his behaviour to Paul after discovering that the latter was a Roman, but he exemplifies the common weakness and indecision of Roman administration in the provinces, the unwillingness of officials to bear responsibility, and their readiness to please the populace even at the price of serious injustice to an unpopular individual. We see the same qualities in Felix's handling of the matter during the next two years (combined in his case with baser motives), and in Pilate's conduct at the trial of Jesus.

On the fifth day the Jews reached Cæsarea, bringing with them a professional legal pleader named Tertullus to conduct the case. The hearing took place on the twelfth day after Paul had reached Jerusalem.

The ample space which the historian devotes to this brief period is unique in the Acts, and shows his sense of the critical importance of what was now occurring. There is nothing approaching to it in the whole book except the proceedings regarding Cornelius and the account of Paul's voyage from Syria to Rome. To understand the character of Luke and his conception of a historian's task, the student must study with special care those three episodes in their relation to the plan of the work as a whole.

The arrangement of the events during these twelve days is not unimportant; yet accurate apportionment is difficult owing to the fact that ancient writers and ancient society were not so careful as we in modern days are forced to be about matters of time, whether in regard to days or hours. Business habits, strict punctuality and strict reckoning of time are modern and Western, not ancient and Oriental.

The probable arrangement of the twelve days is as follows. We take it that Paul reached Jerusalem just after sunset, so that according to Jewish reckoning this occurred in the same day as his visit to James on the following morning.

1. Reception by James and the elders: first day of purification.

2-4. Second, third and fourth days of purification.

5. Fifth day of purification: riot: Paul's speech on the castle stairs.

6. Meeting of the Council (Paul's dream during the night following).

7. Plot to slay Paul is arranged.

8. He starts for Cæsarea before midnight, and reaches Antipatris before dawn: Ananias learns of Paul's departure: first of the five days (XXIV. 1).

9. Paul is handed over to the Procurator Felix in Cæsarea: second day.

10-11. Paul in Cæsarea: third and fourth days.

12. Fifth day: arrival of Ananias and Tertullus in Cæsarea: Paul denounced and the investigation begun.

In the investigation held on the twelfth day by Felix, Tertullus stated the case for the prosecution. According to the rules prescribed in the ancient schools of oratory he began his speech with an elaborate compliment to the governor, designed to conciliate his favour; and in complimenting him on the excellence of his administration, the orator went far beyond the limits of truth. Felix had in reality been an exceptionally bad governor; and two years later the Jews complained to Nero about his conduct, and he was recalled.

Tertullus next stated the charges against Paul. They are three. (1) Paul had been a cause of disorder and sedition among the Jews throughout the Roman world. This charge is a clever misrepresentation of the fact that serious differences of opinion among the Jews, sometimes ending in riot, had occurred in many of the cities which Paul had visited; but it hides the truth, that the troubles had always been originated by Paul's opponents, and that his friends had been unresisting sufferers. Still it was a dangerous charge, considering the character of most Roman officials, who were bent on keeping things quiet at almost any cost.

(2) Paul was a leader of the Nazarean heresy. This was not a serious charge: the Romans had no desire to interfere between one Jewish sect and another: the accusation is made only to lead on to the next charge.

(3) Paul had profaned the holy place. The Romans had legalized the Jewish ritual and recognized any outrage against its ordinances as a crime. The profanation of the holy place would be a serious outrage, but it would depend greatly on the

character of the individual Roman governor what view he would take of the offence. In practice the Romans generally would have winked at even the murder of such a criminal by an infuriated mob, if he were caught in the act and punished at the moment. But, later, when momentary passion had passed and the crime was tried in a court, few Romans would have treated it as very grave.

The weak part of Tertullus's case was that he produced no evidence to support his charges. The accusers were there, but they had no witnesses: they merely asked Felix to question Paul and judge from the answers.

Paul in his reply fastened on this weakness. Like Tertullus, he began with a compliment to the governor, but, unlike Tertullus, he restricted himself to the truth Felix had governed the Jews for many years, and the prisoner might fairly congratulate himself (as he did) on speaking before a judge who knew the law. He denied that he had ever carried on any discussion with anyone in the temple, much less provoked riot there or in any part of the city; and he challenged his accusers to produce any evidence of their first charge. To the second charge he pleaded guilty; but pointed out that to be a Christian implied full acceptance of the whole Jewish Scriptures, both the Law and the

Prophets, full confidence in the hope of the Messiah and of the Resurrection, and perfect innocence and good conscience towards God and men. The third charge he denied absolutely.

The answer was complete and, in the absence of witnesses to support the charges, conclusive. Luke mentions that Felix had a comparatively correct knowledge about Christianity, i.e. he knew in what relation it stood to the Roman law. This remarkable statement plainly shows that a Roman governor had already, when this first case came before him, a fairly exact notion what view Roman law took of the new Faith: in other words, the precedent created by Gallio in Corinth expressed the official Roman opinion: Roman administration refused to regard the preaching of the new Faith as a crime.

Felix, however, would not take the responsibility of offending the Jews merely to do justice to a single person. He postponed the trial for further evidence, thus giving the Jews another chance, though at the same time he showed every indulgence to Paul, consistent with safe custody. He even listened to Paul's preaching and, vicious and corrupt as he was, trembled at the thought of the coming Judgment, yet his terror did not prevent his hoping that Paul might offer a bribe to buy release and freedom. As Felix was a man of high position and wealth, brother of the richest man in Rome,[1] and husband of a princess, he could not have thought of a paltry bribe. Paul's antecedents and position (of which a corrupt ruler certainly informed himself carefully) suggested the hope of a bribe such as Felix would care to accept. This is a proof beyond question that Paul was believed by the governor to have command of considerable wealth. Men like Felix do not mistake a pauper for a wealthy man.

This state of easy custody lasted for two full years, until the beginning of summer A.D. 59. We cannot suppose that Paul spent the time in idleness, but no record is preserved, except that (on our view) the Epistle to the Hebrews was written in 59 by Philip and the Church in Cæsarea, under the direction of Paul, but in Philip's own words (except that Paul himself added the last few verses).

[1] Pallas, the millionaire freedman of the Emperor Claudius.

XLIV

PAUL'S APPEAL TO CÆSAR

Acts XXV. and XXVI.

WHEN two full years had passed over Paul's head in light and privileged confinement, Felix was recalled to Rome on account of the complaints made by the Jews against his greed and injustice; and being desirous of propitiating his enemies by some concession, especially one which cost him nothing, he left Paul in prison.

Festus, the new Governor, arrived in Cæsarea during the summer of A.D. 59. He at once made a brief visit to Jerusalem, where the Jews petitioned him to bring up Paul for trial; but he resolved first to investigate the case in Cæsarea, before granting their wish to have the trial in Jerusalem.

Again there was enacted a scene similar to the trial before Felix two years previously, the Jews accusing Paul and bringing many charges against him without any witnesses to prove their case.

We observe, here, that the Jews stood on a far higher plane of morality than most Asiatic peoples. Embittered against Paul as they were, they made no attempt to bring forward invented evidence. In trials there was some respect for truth. Even the "false witnesses" who gave evidence against Stephen and against Jesus did not invent words which had never been used by the accused; they testified to words which had been spoken, but which were misinterpreted and misunderstood by the witnesses and by all the Jews The Hebrew people had many serious faults, but it is right to acknowledge that morally they had advanced far above their neighbours. The law of Moses had produced an effect on the race. They were self-righteous and hard, but they aimed at righteousness of a narrow yet real kind. The law had been to them a schoolmaster, as Paul calls it, and had placed them on a moral platform fitted to bear the superstructure of true Christianity, whereas the pagan converts had no such platform of moral custom and education to stand upon, and Paul had often occasion to be horrified at the hideous crimes into which they could fall when they stumbled. It was slow work to build up this needed foundation of morality in the pagan cities.

At the new inquiry Paul again denied the charges, and when Festus asked him if he were willing to go to Jerusalem and take trial there, he appealed to Cæsar: in other words, he claimed to be tried before the supreme tribunal of the Empire, over which the Emperor, or more commonly a judge acting for the Emperor, would preside. Festus, after conferring with his legal advisers, granted this appeal, and remitted the case to the highest court of the Roman State. Here again we have clear proof that Paul was considered by the Roman officials in Cæsarea to be a person of standing and therefore of some wealth. The Roman Governor would not send up for trial before the Imperial tribunal any and every person who chose to appeal. He had to judge first of all whether the case and the person was of sufficient importance to be sent on to Rome, for he had himself full authority to judge and to condemn or acquit in such cases as this.

How did it come about that Paul, who in the cities of Asia and Europe had maintained himself by the labour of his hands, appeared now a Roman of rank, believed by Felix to be able to offer a bribe worthy of a rich man's acceptance, and regarded by Festus as one whose appeal to Cæsar must be forthwith accepted? Surely we must understand that formerly he had voluntarily chosen to teach and exemplify the dignity of labour, that he had deliberately elected to be a missionary in the sense that Jesus had ordered, taking no purse with him as he travelled and preached, and rarely even accepting food unless it was earned by his own labour: Philippi, with its generous hospitality and its twice repeated gifts of money when he was in Thessalonica, being the solitary exception which he allowed, and that only when he was constrained by pressing kindness. Now had come the time for a different policy. He had gone to Jerusalem; he had faced death there; and he had received the Divine instruction that he must bear witness to the Faith in Rome. Towards Rome his face was set. His trial must be decided there, and not in Jerusalem. He must appeal to Cæsar, and in the metropolis of the world before the supreme tribunal he must plead the cause of God and of the Church, hoping to gain a charter of freedom for the free preaching of the Gospel in every city of the whole Empire. To gain this charter his rights as a Roman citizen, and as a member of the governing aristocracy of the Roman world, formed the apparent means. Only as a Roman could he be sent up to the Imperial tribunal. Accordingly, he adopted at this crisis a different line of conduct from that which he had pursued on his missionary journeys; and in all parts of his life alike he acted with the same noble spirit.

Before the Roman journey Paul had still to

undergo one more trial, and to speak in the presence of Kings and Governors. Agrippa II with his sister Bernice came to pay a visit of state to the new Governor; and Festus took the opportunity of examining Paul with the assistance of Agrippa's intimate knowledge of Hebrew law and religion. He had to send up a report to the Emperor in the case of this prisoner, and he was puzzled to specify correctly the exact nature of the charges, which only a Jew by religion could properly understand.

In the examination Agrippa, as a King, took precedence and conducted the proceedings, while Festus sat beside him: "Agrippa said unto Paul, Thou art permitted to speak for thyself". The prisoner with an orator's gesture, fettered as he was, addressed the King with the dignity and self-possession that was his birthright, without servility and yet with courtly deference. Beginning by paying a compliment to the King's familiarity with "the customs and questions which are among the Jews," he said only what was true, but he said it with polished and graceful courtesy.

Paul's speech included a brief autobiography, in which he touched summarily on the chief events of his life, and more fully, yet still very briefly, on the epoch-making occasion of his conversion. The apparent differences from the accounts given of this critical event in Chapters IX. and XXII. arise chiefly from the fact that none of the accounts gives every detail, and that different details are mentioned in each case according to the different purpose and emotion of the narrator and the different character of the persons addressed. Here, for example, where Paul was speaking in a Gentile court, he makes no reference to Ananias, because it would not produce any effect on the audience to hear what part an obscure Jew at Damascus had played in the action, whereas that part of the story was likely to appeal strongly to the Jewish auditors in Chapter XXII.

Paul also laid strong emphasis on the promise of the Messiah, the hope of the twelve tribes, and the fact that this hope can be attained only through the raising of the dead. He first mentions this truth in more general terms early in his speech; and then at a later point expounds the fulfilment of the promise in the Death and Resurrection of Jesus.

This idea of the resurrection seemed so absurd and incredible to the rough and blunt Roman officer, that he rudely interrupted the speaker by loudly calling out, " Paul, you may be a great philosopher, but you have no common sense ". Festus had no prejudice against Paul; but regarded him with good-humoured contempt as an unpractical enthusiast. From the Roman Governor Paul turned with a courteous negative to the King, who knew Judea and what had happened there, and boldly put the question to him whether he, who claimed to be a Jew, believed the prophets Agrippa did not like the question. He kept his Judaism for the Jews, but was not willing to display it in a Gentile court. He would not answer the question directly, for if he replied in the affirmative he would incur the ridicule of the Romans, and if he answered in the negative he would sacrifice his reputation with the Jews. He therefore turned aside the question by a half-jesting, half-ironical remark · "You expect to make a Christian of me in very quick time".

The universal opinion of the court was that Paul was not guilty. He might be a hair-brained enthusiast, but he was not a criminal; and Agrippa declared that he might have been set at liberty, had the case not passed beyond their jurisdiction through the prisoner's appeal to Cæsar. Thus it came about that, instead of being released, Paul, though practically acquitted, was through his own demand sent on to "bear witness also at Rome".

The emphatic declaration of Paul's innocence with which the long proceedings in Palestine ended is noteworthy. Luke is careful to record that time after time the Roman officials, such as Gallio, justified Paul and took his part against the Jews; and he alone among the Evangelists records Pilate's thrice-repeated statement acquitting Jesus of all faults before the law (whereas Mark omits it wholly, John and Matthew mention only one occasion).

XLV

PAUL TAKES COMMAND WHEN DANGER THREATENS

Acts XXVII. 1-26

WHEN the decision had been ratified by the agreement of the Roman Procurator and the Jewish King that Paul's appeal to the supreme Imperial tribunal must be accepted and his case sent on to Rome for judgment, it is evident that no further time was lost. Festus had reached Palestine, probably, early in the summer; but the process had dragged on for some considerable time, and the autumn was now approaching or perhaps had begun.

The lateness of the season affected the choice of route. The quickest and least fatiguing way was by sea; but for many months between late autumn and early spring long voyages ceased and what may be called ocean-going ships lay up (though there was no season when ships could not be hired to take short voyages, watching for a fair opportunity). During the season when distant navigation was avoided, the journey from the East to Rome was performed by land through Galatia, Asia, Philippi and Thessalonica.

On these customs in regard to the way of travelling the whole of Paul's voyage turned. The end of the settled season, when the Mediterranean is continuously suited for sailing vessels, was close at hand, and there was every probability that the land route would have to be chosen for part of the way. The centurion Julius, into whose charge Paul was put with a number of other prisoners, took passage in a ship bound for Adramyttium on the coast of Asia. If no better opportunity occurred by the way, it would be easy to get a passage across to Neapolis (XVI 11), and thence the convoy would take the land route. The other prisoners were, as a rule, doubtless criminals, who were being taken to Rome to amuse by their death in the arena the idle populace, habituated to enjoy such cruel sights. Few persons had, like Paul, the distinction of being remitted for trial to the highest court of the Empire.

The prevailing winds on the open Mediterranean throughout the summer are westerly, favouring the voyage from Italy to Egypt and Syria, but making the return voyage difficult. The only way to sail from Cæsarea to Italy or to Adramyttium was to keep close to the coast, and take advantage of the local breezes to dodge along from point to point as a chance occurred. Such voyages were often extremely slow, and at the best many days and much patience were needed to reach the south-western corner of Asia Minor.

In the harbour of Myra, the Lycian city, there happened a favourable chance. One of the large ships which carried corn (v. 38) from Egypt to feed the vast population of the great city of Rome had put in there; and the centurion seized the opportunity, and transferred his whole company of prisoners and guards to this vessel, which was sailing direct to Puteoli on the west coast of Italy, the harbour of Rome. The course of this ship would coincide with that of the other as far as Cnidus; but the Egyptian corn-vessels were the largest and best equipped at that time. This vessel was for some reason belated, and had not accompanied the Egyptian fleet, which sailed in a great body for Puteoli earlier in the year.

The winds continued adverse, and many days elapsed before Cnidus, a promontory on the south-west of Asia Minor, was reached. Hence the vessel would in ordinary course have run across the Ægean Sea north of Crete to the southern point of Greece; but strong north winds were blowing, and there was danger that the ship might be driven on the north coast of Crete, where there are hardly any harbours (except Suda Bay). Accordingly, they ran for shelter under the south coast of Crete; and again began the process of slowly making their way westward from point to point as far as Fair Havens, a harbour near the middle of the long Cretan southern shore.

Here Paul advised that they should lay up for the winter, as the middle of October was now on them. Julius had from the outset treated Paul with great courtesy, because the latter was a person of distinction, not a criminal; and hence the rather strange situation that a prisoner should be offering advice about the conduct of a Roman officer and the management of the ship. Naturally and reasonably, the officer preferred to be guided by the captain and the sailing master, and chose on their advice to pass the winter season further west in the harbour called Phœnix. It was now accepted by all that it was too late to tempt the open sea, and that the winter must be spent in a Cretan port; but Phœnix was the one preferred in such cases (as we know from an inscription recording the detention there of another vessel of the same class), and the navigating authorities thought that they could reach it safely. To us it seems strange that the decision should lie with the soldier and not with the sailors; but the centurion travelling on the Emperor's service commanded even the captain.

Taking advantage, one day, of a gentle south wind, they sailed from Fair Havens; close to the west lay a prominent cape which they had to pass; and it was not quite certain that they could round it with the wind from the south. Paul and Luke were on deck watching, and doubtless all the sailors and prisoners were doing the same. It was an anxious voyage at that late season; and there was the danger that the south wind might cast them on shore. Luke says that they were "close in shore": the record of such a detail reflects the anxiety felt at this moment by one who knew what Paul's advice had been. They passed the cape, and then they had to run to Phœnix across a great bay, where they were much further from shore.

Then the southerly breeze suddenly changed to a north-north-east gale—a change which is frequent on that coast. So strong was the wind that the ship could not keep her course, but had to run before it, thus getting dangerously far out to sea in this stormy season. A modern sailing ship prefers the open sea; but ancient vessels were not so strongly built, and were fitted with one mast and one huge sail, which strained the hull so severely as often to cause leaks and foundering. The little boat, which in calm weather was towed behind the stern, was now hauled on board with difficulty. Another danger threatened: the gale was blowing the ship direct towards the African quicksands: they therefore lowered the yard, and under a little sail with prow turned up towards the wind drifted westward for fourteen days. The ship was leaking, and everything that could be thrown overboard was sacrificed to keep her afloat.

In this time of fear Paul cheered the ship's company by telling of the vision which he had, in which God promised that all on board should be saved. It is noteworthy that in Fair Havens he intimated that there would be much loss of life. Luke does not hesitate to record on that occasion a forecast that proved incorrect: even Paul could be mistaken, and only through direct revelation did he learn the truth. Now in the time of despair and despondency, Paul alone stands out to encourage the crew and to rouse all on board to exert themselves and save themselves. The centurion and the captain pass out of notice, and Paul issues orders.

XLVI

PAUL THE SAVIOUR OF HIS COMPANIONS

Acts XXVII. 27-XXVIII. 10

IN the fourteenth night, as they drifted over the sea Adria, the quick sense of the sailors made them aware that land was near; and soundings showed first a depth of twenty and soon afterwards of fifteen fathoms They therefore anchored by the stern, to avoid running on shore in the dark, and prayed for day. The sailors now got out the boat, pretending to be about to lay out anchors from the prow, but really intending to make their escape. But Paul, perceiving their intention, warned the centurion and the soldiers, who cut the boat adrift. At daybreak, when the time for exertion was approaching and strength was needed, Paul entreated all to take food, and set the example himself. The terms in which his hurried meal is described are evidently chosen to suggest the Eucharist: " when he had taken bread, he gave thanks to God in the presence of all, and he brake it". While it was not in the strict sense a celebration of the sacrament, since almost the whole company were pagans, Luke felt that there was power and blessing in the act. Thus all were encouraged to eat.

The total number of persons on board was 276. The convoy of prisoners must have been large, and the crew in one of the great corn-ships was also numerous: this shows that not the entire crew, but merely one lot of sailors, had been guilty of the cowardly action of attempting to desert the ship.

As the daylight broke, they saw before them an unknown shore, a bay with a sandy beach in one part; and they resolved to run on the beach, casting off the anchors, unfastening the two rudders (which had been lashed up during the night), and hoisting a small foresail to enable them to beach the ship on the most suitable spot. This spot, as they came closer, was seen to be a bank where two seas met, i.e. where a narrow spit of land stretches out from the main island towards a small island, which protects the bay on the west, leaving a narrow channel between the sea on one side and the sea on the other side. On the extremity of this spit, they struck a muddy bottom, into which the prow fixed itself, while the stern was free and beaten by the waves, until it began to break up.

From this place all got safe ashore in one way or another. The soldiers who were responsible with their lives if the prisoners escaped, wished to kill them all; but the centurion, desirous of saving Paul, permitted them all to land. Beyond this single reference Luke takes no notice of the other prisoners during the voyage.

This narrative of the voyage and shipwreck has been almost universally recognized as the most vivid and trustworthy account of ancient seamanship that has been preserved, one that could only have been given by an eye-witness and a faithful and accurate observer. We notice that the direct revelation of the Divine will to Paul plays an important part in the action; and there cannot be any doubt that the revelation was one great cause why Luke was so interested in the story as to relate it with this fullness of detail. In virtue of this revelation Paul is depicted on a higher level than ordinary men, advising more skilfully than the sailors, maintaining hope and courage when all were in despair, playing the part of a true Roman in a Roman ship, reverenced even by the Roman officer, and in his single self the saviour of all. Here is a picture such as Luke loves to paint of the triumph of spiritual over material strength. Even Roman soldiers, the best in the world, lost courage, and were saved by the courage of Paul.

Further, Luke describes the voyage at such length in order to concentrate attention on this part of Paul's career. Paul was now about to stand his trial, and the result of his trial before the supreme court of the Empire was that he was acquitted, and a decisive verdict was thus pronounced in favour of free teaching of the Christian Faith. Subsequently, after the verdict was recalled and persecution became the lot of all Christians, Luke recorded the facts of the earlier period, when the Holy Spirit had guided the Church to that great acquittal.

The company now safe on a shore, which (as they soon learned) was the island of Malta, were kindly treated by the rude natives, who kindled a fire for them. Paul, always helpful, gathered an armful of brush-wood and was throwing it on the fire, when a snake roused by the heat came out of the sticks and fastened on his hand, clinging there until Paul shook it off into the fire. The action shows that the snake was a constrictor, and not (as Luke calls it) a viper, which does not occur in Malta. There is found in the island a species of constrictor, in scientific classification either *Coronella Austriaca* or *Leopardinus* (observers differ as to the exact species), which is in appearance so like a viper as to deceive even a skilled naturalist unless he examines it closely; and the action of this species would be exactly what Luke describes. It has teeth, and bites, but the teeth are so small as hardly to draw blood.

The natives thought the snake was venomous and expected to see Paul die in torture; such belief in the venomous nature of really harmless animals is extremely common among rude peoples. They began to moralize on the justice of God, which had singled out this man among the prisoners; he must have been a murderer who deserved to die: the other prisoners could not be so wicked as he was, and though he had escaped the sea yet Divine justice was now punishing his crime. But when time passed and no harm happened to the supposed murderer, they changed their minds and said he was a god Thus Paul's personality dominated all with whom he was brought in contact. The spiritual power was so manifest in him that even the rude natives recognized it.

The leading man of the island, one Poplius, entertained the company hospitably. He would of course make some distinction, and would pay much more attention to the Roman officer and the captain than to the common soldiers, and more to the soldiers than to the prisoners. But Paul was treated among the distinguished guests, and Luke was with him. Either the courtesy that the centurion had all along shown him, or the reputation he had acquired as a god, procured for Paul this special treatment. In return Paul visited the father of Poplius, who was sick of a fever, and after prayer laid his hands on him and healed him. Thereupon other invalids came from all parts of the island, and received medical attention : Luke the physician took part in the treatment of these invalids, and shared in the honours that were bestowed on Paul.

We understand why Paul was everywhere treated with such attentive courtesy, but why was Luke admitted to participate in it and to be everywhere in close company with a prisoner? It was contrary to the Roman custom to permit any friend to accompany a prisoner on his way to Rome In one famous case even a wife was not permitted to accompany her husband, a Roman noble, when he was carried a prisoner to Rome, and she had to hire a vessel to follow him. The only way in which Luke could be allowed to accompany Paul and to be always close to him was that he was understood to be a slave attending on his master Paul. The relation between master and slave was close and familiar, and often very affectionate ; and it was natural and permissible that a confidential slave should attend Paul everywhere.

We notice two marks of accurate detail. (1) The sea between Crete and Malta is called Adria (i.e. Adriatic) ; that was true to sailors' language ; and the name Adriatic was even extended to include all the sea as far as Cyprus on the east and the African coast on the south. (2) Poplius is called the first (man) of the island. This was the technical name for the head man in Malta, as we know from inscriptions.

XLVII

A LAST APPEAL TO THE JEWS

Acts xxviii. 11-31

AT the earliest moment possible, after spending the three months of midwinter in Malta, the convoy of prisoners sailed for Rome. The regular season for navigation had not yet begun, but even in winter it was always possible to take advantage of fair wind and weather, and to sail from point to point as occasion presented itself. Especially was this the case with the large corn-vessels, which maintained the service between Alexandria and Rome. Such ships were used to long voyages across the open sea; and it was important that they should reach Puteoli, the harbour for Rome, as early as possible.

The centurion found one of the corn-ships which had been driven out of its normal course by the autumn storms, just like his previous vessel, but had escaped shipwreck and spent the winter in a Maltese harbour. On a favourable opportunity this ship sailed north to the coast of Sicily; it was detained three days in Syracuse; it reached the Straits of Messina with a wind that was not quite favourable and required careful navigation; it was detained one day in the harbour of Rhegium; then a south wind sprang up, blowing fair for their destination; thus after one whole day and part of the next spent in the long run across the open sea they reached Puteoli, the great harbour of Campania and of the whole Italian west coast, where all the Alexandrian ships discharged their cargo of corn for transport to Rome by land.

The centurion's courtesy allowed Paul seven days' rest in Puteoli; the voyage on an ancient ship was rather trying at the best of times, as none of the comforts which modern vessels offer were available for ordinary passengers: people slept hard and fared poorly, and once Tacitus tells that a regiment of Roman soldiers, after the long voyage to Egypt and back, was disabled for a time from active service even on an occasion of utmost need.

In Puteoli, the harbour for the East, strangers from Syria, Palestine, etc., were numerous; and here the new religion had established itself. Paul enjoyed the hospitality of the brethren, until the journey to Rome was made. He was expected there. His letter to the Romans written from

Corinth three years ago had intimated his intention of visiting the capital of the world, and many of the numerous friends with whom he had come in contact during his wandering life found their way to Rome on business or duty. Now, considering the situation, it seems beyond doubt that a report of the case with reasons for sending on the appeal to the supreme court, must have been dispatched by Festus to Rome; the report would be sent by Imperial courier along the land route. With a fortunate voyage the centurion would have reached Rome before the courier, and probably a copy of the report was sent in his charge; but, as it happened, the courier must have arrived long before the centurion. Further, there can be no doubt that the brethren in Rome were in communication with those in the East, and heard from time to time of Paul's fate; the sympathetic interest between the scattered congregations, which was caused by such frequent communication, was the main support of unity, the very life-blood of the Church.

Accordingly when a messenger from Puteoli brought private news to the brethren in Rome that Paul had reached Italy, many of them started to welcome him on the way. Some of these eager friends met him at the "Market of Appius," forty-three miles from Rome, some at the "Three

Shops," about thirty-three miles. The sight of those friendly faces cheered Paul, and he thanked God. In spite of alleviating circumstances and the Divine encouragement, the strain and hardship of the voyage must have told on his delicate frame, and physical weakness caused low spirits. We see in his letters written from Rome plain signs how much his nature longed for sympathetic friends; and we can imagine the joy which he felt when his Roman friends, some known to him of old, some new, greeted his arrival in these two wayside towns.

On reaching Rome, Paul rested three days—such a long holiday is a plain proof of his fatigue and weakness—and then invited the principal Jews to the house which he had hired, and where he lived under guard of a soldier. He explained his case to them in as polite a way as was consistent with truth: he was delivered to the Romans (he avoids saying that the Jews did this); the Roman authorities found him innocent and wished to release him; then as the Jews opposed his release, he had been forced to appeal to Cæsar, but not in any spirit of revenge or accusation against his nation. And now, having come to Rome, his first act was to entreat his own people to speak with him; the Promise made by God to His people, the Hope of His people, drove him on into imprisonment, into chains, and now to entreat the Jews in Rome.

They answered that they knew nothing about the case. It is impossible to believe that they spoke the whole truth; but they were evidently nonplussed at this unexpected situation, and astounded at the devotion of Paul to his cause and to his nation. The man whom the Jews had sought to kill first with their hands, afterwards with all the weapons of legal procedure, felt no bitterness against his persecutors: they sought to kill him: he only sought in return to save them. These Roman Jews began to wonder whether they had heard all the truth They would not betray their own people, but for the present would merely listen to what Paul had to say for himself. They denied that they had received any letter from Judea about him: it is hard to believe that this can be true: the statement is probably an evasion, to which some colour of justification could be given in a sidelong fashion. They denied that any of their nation had reported or spoken any harm of Paul: this is even harder to credit; many a pilgrim must have returned and told the tale in Rome; but in some evasive way also they could maintain that no harm had been told of Paul. They acknowledged that they had heard much about the new sect on all hands, and that the accounts were all hostile; but they were prepared to hear from Paul himself what he had to say in its defence. They made no allusion to the existence of Christians in Rome; yet they must have been well aware that a Roman congregation existed, and that people of their nation belonged to it. The whole brief reply is evasive, false, and superficially polite. Luke felt this; he will not point it out, any more than he would draw attention to the incorrectness of the Tribune's statement in XXIII. 27. That was not his method. He states the facts simply and accurately, and expects his readers to understand the situation as he knew it.

On an appointed day many Jews came to Paul's house, and he spent the whole day setting before them the facts about Jesus, proving from Moses and the prophets that He was the Promised Messiah. The result was the usual one: some believed and some disbelieved. The audience departed, and Paul, quoting the words of Isaiah, recognized his failure with the Jews, but added that the Gentiles would hear. The second book of Luke's history ends with this intimation and the general statement that the Apostle continued to preach in his own dwelling freely and boldly for two whole years.

XLVIII

WEAKNESS MADE STRONG: THE AUTOBIOGRAPHY OF A MISSIONARY

2 *Cor.* xi. 18–xii. 10

In his second letter to the Corinthians, protesting against the low opinion which his detractors expressed of him, Paul introduces a short sketch of his own career, prefacing it with an apology for the appearance of egotism and self-glorification, which autobiography necessarily wears. He will describe his own life only because his opponents compel him to describe his services.

His detractors compared him unfavourably with certain Jewish teachers, who had come from Palestine to Corinth. Paul makes the comparison also, and gives it a very different colour. He is as truly a Hebrew, an Israelite, an heir of the Promise, as they. He is far more truly a minister of Christ than they, for he had suffered imprisonment, personal chastisement and risk of death in a way with which they could not compare.

He had been five times beaten by his Jewish

countrymen. These beatings are not mentioned by Luke, but both in Palestine and elsewhere the Jewish communities exercised justice according to their own law on their own people within certain limits. He had been three times beaten with the rods of Roman lictors. This might occur either in a Roman Colony or in any place where he came in contact with a Roman Governor: in Philippi alone is such beating recorded, but the persecution and expulsion which he endured in the Colonies of Antioch and Lystra might well be accompanied with beating. Three times he had suffered shipwreck, and on one of these occasions he had been in the water for a day and a night. These are not mentioned in the Acts (this letter was written before the period described in xx. 4 and following). In his long missionary journeys he had been exposed to many dangers, from flooded rivers, from robbers, in cities and in deserts and at sea, from foreigners and Jews and even, worst of all, from pretended Christians. He had suffered from fatigue and hard work, from want of sleep and food and drink and clothes, from cold and abstinence.

The greatest trial of all was the ceaseless anxiety about his young churches, which always pressed heavy on his heart. He sympathized with all, suffered in their sufferings, denied himself the freedom of life to which he was entitled because some weak and over-scrupulous Christians thought that such freedom of conduct was wrong, and was heart-broken when any of his converts failed in their Christian life. In his weakness he had been saved by the power of God, as when he fled from the Governor of Damascus, and was saved not through his courage but in the refuge of a basket hanging from a wall.

The crowning honour of his career lay in the direct communion with God which had been granted to him. This was a private experience, which lay between him and God, and which in ordinary circumstances he would shrink from mentioning to men. Even to speak of such favours as had been bestowed on him in this way savours of boastfulness; but he speaks now under compulsion. In a vision fourteen years ago he had been transported into heaven; he had heard what he could not repeat; he did not himself fully comprehend what had happened, whether his body was thus caught up, or whether the spirit was set free from the body for a time and enabled to commune with God. Perhaps it was not the man, but the spirit alone, that had seen or heard what occurred in Paradise. Of such honour, in some way that he could not define or describe, had he been found worthy.

It was through his weakness that he was made strong and exalted to honour. He therefore feels justified in glorying in his weakness, because through his weakness he was more fitted to exhibit the power of God, which acted through him and made use of him for great purposes, far beyond his own poor strength to carry into effect.

It has sometimes been thought by modern writers that Luke lays too much stress on the actions and the sufferings of Paul; but this account given by the Apostle himself shows that Luke was reticent, and passed lightly and silently over much that had befallen him. We can only conjecture as to the occasions when many of these events happened, and we cannot fit them exactly into his life. As to the great vision, it was a secret of Paul's spiritual life, mentioned only through this accidental cause. Yet he dates it to a year, a thing that he very rarely does. It occurred in the fourteenth year before he was writing. The Epistle was written in the year 56-57 (i.e. the year beginning, according to Corinthian custom, in autumn 56); and the fourteenth year before that (according to the ancient way of counting) was 43-44. In that year Paul had gone to Jerusalem with Barnabas, and had a vision in the temple, in which he was ordered to go away and begin his mission to the Gentiles. May we not connect the account given to the Corinthians with the other account given in the speech to the Jews, and believe that the order was accompanied with some marvellous revelation regarding the purpose of God, about which he could not speak to men? That this was so suits well with the next words. Lest Paul should become proud through the consciousness of this great revelation, his weakness was brought home to him by the disease from which he soon began to suffer, and which kept always before his mind the knowledge that he could do nothing through his own strength. This disease, the stake in the flesh, which showed the power of Satan over him, began to afflict him not long after he left Jerusalem on that occasion; and, as seems probable, it seized upon him in Pamphylia. But this weakness was the cause of the marvellous success which was granted him immediately afterwards in Galatia: he visited Galatia on account of it, and there he gained the first comprehensive victory of his missionary career. God's power was made perfect in Paul's weakness.

Such seems the thought in this part of the autobiography; and the other autobiography contained in the Epistle to the Galatians ought to be carefully compared with it. Each throws light on the other in instructive fashion; and the nature of Paul's mind is set before us by the two accounts written at different times and in different states of feeling. But in both there is one character : nothing seems of value to Paul in his past history except his relation to God : all else sinks into insignificance in his retrospect. There is nothing real in the world except the Divine ; all else is error and illusion. The greatest things are done through man's weakness . the silence of God shouts aloud among men (to adapt the striking language of Ignatius). the greatest of saints is in himself (as Paul says about himself to Timothy) the chief of sinners.

XLIX

THE LAW OF SPIRITUAL COMPENSATION

2 *Cor.* VIII.

IN his second letter to the Corinthians Paul pleads for a liberal contribution to the fund which he was anxious that all his young Gentile Churches should send to relieve the poor Christians in Jerusalem. In Sections XXXVI and XXXVII the purpose of this contribution, viz. to foster and strengthen the feeling of unity between the Jewish and Gentile congregations, was fully described; and the importance attached to it by Paul was explained. In his first letter, written from Ephesus a good deal more than a year previously (XVI. 1 f.), he had commended this contribution to their attention, quoting the example of the Galatian Churches, and had advised them to lay by every Sunday a proportion of their earnings, so that when he arrived no time need be spent in gathering contributions, and there should be no occasion for him to solicit donations, but the whole matter should proceed from their voluntary action in storing up their weekly subscriptions. Titus, who had visited them in the interval, had again recommended the subject to them. Now during A.D. 56 Paul once more, in view of Titus's approaching second visit, urges them to have everything completed and ready.

It is interesting to observe the arguments by which, not directly but only indirectly, he solicits their contributions. He desired that the collection should be voluntary, but the idea of charitable giving, now so familiar to every Protestant congregation, was then entirely new; and it was necessary to mention the subject, and make the reasons plain to these recently converted pagans of Corinth.

He first quotes the example of the Macedonian Churches, Philippi (which was always generous, Phil. IV. 16), Thessalonica, Beroea, and possibly other more recent foundations (Rom. XV. 19). The Macedonians, who were tried and proved in the furnace of suffering for their faith, showed their happiness in the Christian life amid their deep poverty by giving most liberally. Up to and almost beyond the limits of their power, they contributed voluntarily and unsolicited, even begging to be allowed the opportunity of showing their appreciation of the grace and of joining in the work of helping their fellow-Christians. They not merely gave what Paul had hoped for, viz. money, but they gave themselves in whole-hearted devotion. Titus is now about to visit Corinth again, and Paul trusts that he will carry to completion this gracious act on the part of the Corinthians, as successfully as he had done his work on his first visit; and hopes that they will show themselves as abundant in the grace of charitable giving as they were richly endowed in respect of faith, and power of expressing their inspired thoughts, and knowledge of the truth, and eager devotion, and finally in love for Paul.

The Apostle does not order them to make a contribution; he wishes that their action and their gifts should proceed from their own sense of what was right, and from the generous impulses of their own heart. He only mentions the example set by the generosity of the Macedonian Churches as a test by which the sincerity of the love which the Corinthians felt might be tried.

Then follows one of the most noteworthy sentences in the whole of Paul's writings. In VIII. 9 we have the clearest and most indubitable declaration of the pre-existence of Jesus as God before He condescended to take on himself human form. This is the doctrine which John states with special emphasis: the Word was in the beginning with God: the Word was God: the Word became flesh and dwelt among men. Paul here has the same thought in his mind, and quotes it as a higher example than the Macedonian Churches for Corinth to follow. Jesus voluntarily gave up the riches of His existence and Divine power in heaven, and took on Him the poverty and humbleness of human nature, that the Corinthians through His poverty in life on earth and His death might attain to the spiritual riches of salvation.

A third argument, addressed to the reasoning powers of the Corinthians (on which they rather prided themselves), is that they made a beginning of this collecting in the preceding year, and did so willingly. As they began, it is only reasonable that they complete their own undertaking. It is irrational to begin any enterprise and stop half-way. If they are now suffering from poverty and bad trade and loss of profits, they can, of course, give only in proportion to their means at the moment. Paul advises all men to give only according to what they actually possess, and not as lavishly as if they were wealthy. It is not according to the will of God, or the dictates of reason and justice, to indulge in the false generosity of giving away what one does not really possess: that is giving at the expense of others; true charity consists in giving what one possesses of one's own.

Nor ought one to give away all that one possesses,

and thus reduce oneself to penury and become an object of charity to others. To do that only adds to the burden which the congregation has to support. True religious feeling is rational and sensible; and does not squander all that it has. It thinks, and reasons, and estimates how much it can do, and in what way it can make the best use of its resources for the benefit of all. At the same time the standard of giving should lie in a certain balance and equality. If the Corinthians now give of their abundance to the struggling and poverty-stricken brethren in Jerusalem, the time may come when the latter will have the opportunity from their abundance of helping the Corinthians on some occasion when they are afflicted. Thus the Church of God lives as a single body, all of whose parts are nourished equally and equally healthy, not all doing the same work, but having all their separate duties and functions, each co-operating with the other, each aiding the other, and so all maintaining a harmonious and equable life of strenuous activity.

This healthy condition of the body and of the congregation implies that no part and no person should retain a superabundance; each has what is fair and suitable to maintain efficient work. The case of the healthy Church is similar to what is told in the Old Testament about the congregation of the Hebrews gathering manna for their daily food. No one gained anything by gathering a superabundant store, for he found that nothing remained over after satisfying the wants of his family and himself; and, on the other hand, if anyone found it out of his power to gather a large amount, what he did collect always proved sufficient So in the life of the Christian congregation he that gathers a superabundant store and tries to hoard it, will find that he gains nothing from it. if the Church is in proper health each part supplies the other. Such is the law of spiritual compensation Through the operation of this law great charitable organizations have been built by voluntary unsolicited contributions; such are for example the China Inland Mission and Quarrier's Homes for orphan and destitute children, neither of which has ever sent out any request for aid or for subscriptions. Each has been created by faith and prayer.

L

PAUL'S LAST WILL AND TESTAMENT

2 *Tim.* iv. 1-18

A PATHETIC interest, apart from their intrinsic value, is given to the words of this passage from Paul's last letter, by the circumstances in which they were written. Paul's second trial in Rome before the supreme court had begun; the first hearing was over, and the final stage was postponed for a time. Although the first stage had been successfully passed, yet he had no expectation that the final result would be equally favourable. He felt that the time had come when he must leave his work on earth, his life was already being poured out as an offering to God.

Years had now elapsed since the time which is indicated in Section XLVII. In the interval Paul's first trial had been successfully surmounted. He had revisited the Hellenic Churches round the shores of the Ægean Sea. He had written 1 Timothy and Titus. He had been arrested by

Roman command, and brought to the capital of the Empire for trial.

At the same time the final stage of the trial was not immediately imminent. It had been postponed; and the probable reason for this long delay is that witnesses were to be brought from the scenes of Paul's work in the East, or investigations made there as to its character and effect. Thus arises the double tone in this chapter. It contains instructions to Timothy as to his conduct and work after his master's death, and yet it urges him repeatedly to come to see Paul in Rome (a long journey which might take from one to three months according to the route), and to bring with him books and comforts for use in the winter season.

The interest of the passage for us lies mainly in the former point of view It is the last message of a man who felt that death was approaching · it sums up his own work, and provides for the continuance of that work when he is gone. Paul's instructions, and, as we might almost say, his last will and testament, for the charge which he gives to Timothy is expressed so solemnly and impressively that it may fitly be so called, are characteristic.

Paul's sole concern in view of death is that the work be carried on. He foresees what dangers beset the Church in the future, because those dangers have already begun. Some are weary of "the sound and health-giving doctrine," and their number will in the future be much increased. The teaching, which imparts health and points the way to salvation, is felt to be trite, uninteresting, and old-fashioned, and people are full of curiosity and interest about novelties in teaching: their ears itch for a more alluring and exciting sort of instruction: they want teachers who will advise them to do what they desire to do, and who will tickle their fancy with quaint and clever though false philosophical discourses. Such teaching only diverts people from hearing the truth.

In opposition to this fatal kind of teaching, Paul urges Timothy to preach the Divine message, the true Gospel, as he must be judged hereafter and as he must live now in the sight of God. He should press on the work at all times, not putting off in hope of a more favourable opportunity hereafter, but acting now, whether the moment is favourable or not: he should reprove faults, encourage all to exert themselves, be patient with them, but always teach. He is to take up the work which is now slipping from Paul's hands.

In verse 7 there is a figure of speech which is not military (as the usual translation makes it), but connected with athletic contests: " I have competed in the honourable contest: I have run the race to the finish : I have observed all the rules of this race-course of faith ". In the Christian life the competitor for the prize of righteousness must feel the same intense eagerness and show the same concentration of all his powers on the great effort, as are necessary to win the prize in a great race. The prize for the race was in ancient times a garland, and this garland or crown is ready for Paul as the consummation of his intense and strained effort in life. There is, however, one marked difference between the garland offered for an athletic prize and the garland which God, the fair umpire and judge, will award. Only one can gain the prize in an athletic contest, but all can equally gain that prize of a righteous life, if they are animated with the true love for the appearing of Christ and the coming of His kingdom (verses 1 and 8).

Now appears the human side in Paul's nature. He is lonely, except for the companionship of Luke. Several of his assistants he has sent away on mission work; and Demas, a good Christian in the past, has been unable to endure the danger and trials of companionship with Paul, and has gone back to Thessalonica to enjoy comfort and ease at home. Paul has sent Tychicus to Ephesus to relieve Timothy, and set the latter free to come with Mark to Rome before the winter begins. But another also has gone to Ephesus, an enemy and a danger, Alexander, against whom Paul warns Timothy.

In the first stage of his trial no one supported Paul by his presence and countenance. In reading this statement, however, we must remember that only Roman citizens could appear in court to support him; there is no reason to think that Luke was a Roman citizen (except as a freedman, probably, who was not privileged to appear thus in court), or Tychicus, but in the Roman Church there were some citizens who shrank from the trial, and Paul felt their desertion.

Yet he pleaded his own cause, with Christ as his supporter; and the Divine power had strengthened him so that the cause of the Gospel was set forth in the hearing of that great court, the supreme tribunal of the Empire, and so much effect was produced that the imminent condemnation was postponed. The result was, indeed, not a complete acquittal; but still it was a great triumph that in such a time of persecution,[1] when trial generally resulted in instant condemnation, further investigation was found necessary, and a long postponement was pronounced for the trial. Paul rejoiced in this result, not because he was afraid of death, but because it implied greater freedom for the Christians and fuller opportunity to preach.

[1] This was the persecution of Nero, which began in A.D. 64.

We know what was the usual method at that time of executing criminals who were condemned on such charges as were brought against the Christians. They were frequently exposed to be torn and devoured by wild beasts in the amphitheatre, or their death was otherwise contrived to be an amusement to the brutal populace of Rome; and the expression which Paul uses, "I was delivered out of the mouth of the lion," was probably suggested by this, though he himself as a Roman citizen was privileged to have a more honourable form of death.

LI

THE EPITAPH OF PAUL

2 *Tim.* iv. 7

THESE words, "I have fought the good fight: I have finished the course: I have kept the faith," are the brief review which Paul, in the anticipation of threatening death, makes of his life and his work. They sum up his whole character.

As was stated in Section L. they refer, not to warfare, but to competition in athletic sports. The Hellenic peoples, among whom his Gentile Churches were founded, were very fond of such sports, which formed a recognized part of the education of every boy, and were carefully regulated under trained medical guidance. Victory in the great international competitions was regarded as the highest of distinctions, not merely for the successful athlete, but for the city to which he belonged; and, in that keenly contested arena victory could be gained only by the most intense and concentrated effort, following on a long preliminary period of training according to very severe rules. The rules of the course and of the preparation for it, were rigidly enforced by the judges who regulated the competition and decided the prize. Competitors who had not strictly complied with all the rules were disqualified remorselessly. To win the prize, not merely must one be first, one must attain that position in accordance with stern laws and regulations

In a series of metaphors drawn from this side of Hellenic life, Paul finds the description which will best explain to his readers (not merely Timothy but all the Ephesian Church) the intensity and the long course of concentrated application which characterized his life and the life of every Christian: "I have competed in the honourable contest: I have run the race to the winning post: I have observed the rules which regulate the race-course of faith". Paul was the typical man, the typical human Christian. Our life, just like his, must be one long struggle onwards towards a goal. We can maintain the struggle only by strict discipline, and the observing of all the rules, as he did. We reach the goal and win the prize only in the hour of death, as he reached it. The struggle ends only with our life: it must be maintained to the end. The prize is not in this life or of this life; but it can be won by all who persevere to the last.

Such is the whole life of Paul. He was an eager competitor from the beginning to the end. Before he learned what Christ was, when he hated Him and persecuted all His followers, he was already struggling on in his ignorance and blindness towards the knowledge of God and of truth He was even then a leader of men, a preacher, a missionary, eagerly bent on bringing others to the truth as he believed it. On the road to Damascus, near that city, he saw with his own eyes the Jesus still living whom he had believed to be a dead impostor. The direction of his efforts was changed from that time onwards. He knew now where the truth lay; and the same devouring enthusiasm, the same concentrated energy, which he had before ignorantly applied in a misdirected course, he now applied to the spreading of his better knowledge. He had to face a constant succession of difficulties, as we must in our life. He was always misunderstood and suspected by many, as the strenuous reformer will always be. But he always found devoted and zealous friends, as the true and honest seeker after knowledge always finds them, friends ready to guarantee his honesty with their credit and their life, ready to believe in him even where appearances were against him, and to help him in all his difficulties. All men who work unselfishly for the good of the world, all who try to achieve something noble and generous in their life, all who live for a high ideal, will turn with growing interest and admiration to the career of Paul, and will find mirrored in it the best side of their own nature.

When he first came to Jerusalem after his conversion, the disciples were afraid of him, for they could not believe in his truth. Barnabas helped him, became his champion, and guaranteed his good faith. Then he disputed against the Hellenist Jews, his own former friends (since he, too, was a Hellenist Jew); but they went about to slay him. He had to flee from Jerusalem. He lived many years a life that was undistinguished, while he was learning the Christian missionary's life by living it, the only way in which it can be learned. This was his apprenticeship, in which there seems to have been little apparent external success, for Luke records nothing. At last Barnabas brought him to Antioch, and there he found friends and associates, but still he ranked last among the Antiochian leaders. He was then sent forth by the Spirit along with Barnabas to a new work in the West; and in the prosecution of this work he had to part from that dear and tried friend, who was not prepared to do all that Paul believed necessary for success in their joint career. He had to choose between his work and companionship with his best friend. He chose his work; but the cost was great.

This is the sorest trial of human life. It is not only our unsympathetic opponents who misunderstand us. Sometimes even our friends differ from us, disagree with our views, suspect and disapprove of our aims and course of life, and part from us. We have to choose between friendship and truth, the hardest choice in life. Are we quite sure that we are right in our view? May we not have mistaken our course? Shall we be justified in breaking the bond of true companionship? With that question comes doubt and anxiety, perplexity and almost despair.

As we see that Paul's life mirrors our trials and struggles, so also we may hope to gain some of his consolations and rewards. He attained to many revelations of the nature and will of God. In those revelations he found the highest glory of his earthly life They were a sacred possession of which he could not speak much, but which he kept deep hidden in his heart. We are not denied such revelations. We, too, may have moments of insight and inspiration, in which we attain to direct communion with the Divine Nature, and to sympathy with the purpose and will of God—moments in which the Truth seems to unveil itself to our gaze. Those moments are brief and interrupted. We cannot remain long on that high level; but we see that to Paul also those moments of inspiration were discontinuous. The prize, the crown of life, came to him only with death.

While we see in Paul the man who struggled through error towards truth, we recognize in him also the highest type of man. We never understand him until we begin to judge his conduct on the highest plane of human action. If we look on him from this point of view, then the longer we study him the better we appreciate the loftiness of his motives, his unselfishness, his noble and generous spirit in judging the world, his frankness in condemning all wrong-doing and wrong-thinking, his courtesy and delicate consideration for the feelings of others, his patience in pleading with them.

LII

REVIEW OF THE INFLUENCE OF LOCAL CIRCUMSTANCES ON THE LIFE OF PAUL

TARSUS lay in the lowlands of Cilicia, less than eighty feet above the level of the sea, from which it was distant about ten miles down the River Cydnus. The Cydnus has now changed its course and flows east of, instead of through, the city; and only small boats can cross the bar and enter the river. Careful engineering operations were needed to keep the channel clear and deep, so that ships could sail up into the heart of Tarsus; and a lagoon, through which the river flowed before reaching the sea, was embanked and made useful as the principal harbour and arsenal of the city. Moreover, a road was cut and built to the north over the Taurus Mountains, and the Cilician Gates were opened to trade. Thus through the energy, forethought and skill of its inhabitants, Tarsus was placed at the point where sea-going ships could best profit by the trade which poured down from central Asia Minor toward the nearest and easiest outlet.

This advantage, we must note, was not the free gift of nature, but was gained by the application of knowledge and hard work. The country has now relapsed into its natural condition, and is dreary, repellent, and in large part marshy, but, by draining and by navigation works on the river, a great extent of fertile soil was formerly made available for agriculture. The ancient accounts tell with what pride the Tarsians regarded their river. It was not beautiful, and strangers who sailed up to Tarsus could only wonder at the Tarsian feeling; but the people loved it because it was, so to say, their own offspring, created by their skill and energy. They had transformed a dreary stretch of half-inundated lands, fringed by sand-heaps on the shore, into a rich plain, holding in its bosom a great city through which ran a river able to float the merchandise of many lands—a city with its feet resting on a great inland harbour and its head reaching up to the hills. The pride of the Tarsians in their city, noted by ancient travellers, was deep-rooted in their nature; and it appears in Paul, at one of the most dangerous moments of his life, when, bruised, beaten, and at the point of death, he was barely rescued from a fanatical

Jewish mob by Roman soldiers. At that moment, when his life was dependent on the discipline of the soldiers and on the goodwill of their commander, we cannot suppose that in answering the hurried questions put to him he would indulge in mere picturesque details. He said, "I am a Jew, a Tarsian of Cilicia, citizen of no mean city". In that scene Paul showed extraordinary courage and coolness, and seized the first possible opportunity to address the mob which a few minutes before had been tearing him in pieces; but the fact that he called himself, not a Roman (as he did immediately after, using the title which was most honourable and most likely to move the Tribune), but a Tarsian, and praised the importance of Tarsus, cannot be satisfactorily explained except because he shared in the feelings of the Tarsians among whom he had been born and educated. In modern times a Jew may be a patriotic Frenchman or a good Englishman, according to his birth, and yet remain a convinced and loyal Jew; and there is no reason, except modern prejudice, to think it anything but natural that Paul should entertain a deep and tender feeling for the home of his childhood, in which his family had held an honourable place for generations.

To his Tarsian education, also, Paul owed it that he could move in Hellenic society at his ease, comprehending and adapting himself to it as one to the manner born, knowing instinctively what Hellenes thought and felt and desired He was never quite a foreigner among Hellenes. This was an immense advantage in the Hellenic world, and fitted him to be the Apostle of the cities round the Ægean Sea. Moreover he was born a Roman citizen, with all the privileges of the race that governed the world. Several times, in occasions of need, this privilege (which belonged only to a few distinguished Tarsian families) helped him to triumph over apparently insuperable difficulties. It gave him the right to appeal to the Emperor, and thus to "bear witness also at Rome" and to "stand before Cæsar"; and it qualified him to look forward to preaching the Gospel even in Spain, where he must speak in Latin, and to aspire to conquer not merely the Hellenic East, but also the Latin West. Thus, even before his birth, he had been fitted by the circumstances of his family and ancestry to be the Apostle of the Gentiles (Gal. I. 15), to interpret to the outer world the religion that had been nursed among the Jews. There is no good missionary who does not often feel how hard it is to comprehend the foreign people whom he addresses, and what difficulty is thrown in his path by the fact that he is a stranger to the heart and thoughts and hopes of his hearers

Paul was free from this difficulty; and his freedom from it is conspicuous in many scenes of his life.

It was in Tarsus, too, that he had learned to understand the popular paganism, to know that there were certain fundamental ideas of good (Rom. II. 14 f.) amid the vast edifice of abomination that overspread and concealed the good, and to hate with the whole passionate fervour of his mind the idolatry, the false conception of God's nature, which had destroyed the possibility of improvement and nearer approach to God in the votaries of the Anatolian rites.

In Tarsus, again, more fully than in any other city, there was a synthesis between Grecian and Oriental manners and ideas. The beginnings had been worked out of a peaceable amalgamation of European and Asiatic in a system that was neither purely Greek nor purely Oriental. Throughout all history, both ancient and modern, the contact and intercourse between the active peoples of the Western and the more receptive Eastern races has stimulated the most fruitful developments of life, but the contact has generally taken the form of war and hatred. In Tarsus, better than in any other ancient city, the problem of co-operation had been solved in a peaceful association of the two elements.

Among many signs of the influence exerted on

Paul by his Tarsian upbringing, one more may be touched here. It is a fact of human nature that a man can only with difficulty emancipate himself from early prepossessions regarding the conduct of women in society. Paul was accustomed in Tarsus to the complete veiling of women, who there walked the streets wholly covered up from view, like Turkish ladies in more recent times. In his attitude toward women he moves between two extremes. On the one hand, he knew that in the fully developed Christian Church, as it shall be, there is no distinction of nationality or rank or sex, but that all are placed on an equality and made one in Christ. But on the other hand, he knew only too well that his congregations stood in grave need of improvement, and had not yet risen far above their pagan standard of life. He felt that the reputation of the Church in pagan society, as well as its future development, depended largely on the conduct of its women. He was always anxious about them; he was firmly persuaded that it was unwise for Christian women to go far outside of current views as to propriety; and it seems beyond doubt that his early prepossessions influenced in some degree the advice which he gave, and the rules that he prescribed, about the conduct and the veiling of women. All must feel that he was right in saying that the rule ought to be a mean and balance between the Christian freedom of the future and the conventions of present society ; but we must remember that he regarded the present rule as different from the truth of the future.

In his early youth Paul chose his life. There was open to him the career of a citizen in the Empire, such as many good Jews (as well as bad ones) had followed ; but he chose the religious life after the type of the old prophets. He would not remain among his Tarsian countrymen, serve the state, marry, and build up a family: he would follow the Divine life, and he went to Jerusalem as its proper environment, to study the Law at the feet of its greatest living teacher. For many years he lived in Jerusalem ; and its influence on him was profound. But this influence cannot here be touched, because to touch it is to describe the whole basis of his character. Paul was fundamentally the Hebrew. All other influences were modifying and secondary, they enriched and varied and sweetened the Hebrew type, and hence they can be briefly described. But Jerusalem, first as dreamed of in Tarsus, afterwards as his environment for many years, made the fabric of Paul's mind.

Damascus and Arabia touched him ; but the next city which strongly influenced him was Syrian Antioch. There, however, it was apparently not the city as a whole, but the Christian congregation and its leaders, which moulded him. Contact with the gracious, sympathetic, and generous nature of Barnabas was an education in itself. The other leaders were to him revered figures, to whose example he must mould his conduct. He was still learning: the period for command had not yet begun. In Antioch the Church grew among the Gentiles, but did not directly go to them: it welcomed them through the door of the synagogue. Corresponding to this isolation of the Church from the city is the faintness of the impression which Antioch makes on the pages of Luke. The congregation and its leaders, a harmonious and impressive body, stand out before us; but no impression of the city is conveyed, except that it was at some distance from the sea, and that Paul went down to Seleucia to take ship for Cyprus.

Paphos presents itself as the seat of a Roman Governor, whose court furnished a memorable scene, a real turning-point in Paul's life. Here first he stepped forward as the leader, and spoke directly to a Gentile as such. The decisive step was begun, and could never be retraced; but its effects were not apparent in Paphos itself.

Perga, the capital of Pamphylia, appears only in passing, once and again. No work was done here on the first visit, but the Divine power directed

Paul, through the weakness and bodily infirmity which affected him, to the real beginning of his proper work. He went across Taurus, a long and dangerous journey, full of perils of rivers and robbers, to Pisidian Antioch; and there achieved instantaneous and marvellous success. Within twelve days almost the whole city was listening to him, and he had turned from the Jews to the Gentiles. Antioch was a Roman Colony, the governing city of the southern half of the great province Galatia, military centre for defence against the still dangerous tribes of the Taurus Mountains, lying on the skirts of the Sultan Dagh, 3500 feet above sea-level. Its people shared in the pride of Roman authority, although the mass of them had not the full privilege of Roman citizens. Paul did not appear among them as the aristocratic Roman, but as a poor, weak stranger, suffering from an illness which tried their hearts, because it was believed to be a punishment inflicted by Divine power on persons accursed. Yet they did not despise him from the height of their colonial dignity; but received him forthwith as the messenger of God. Not the whole city, however, welcomed Paul; a part held aloof; and this part was doubtless the Roman aristocracy, more dignified, more difficult to move, and not reached by the same address as the older population, for the latter spoke Greek, in which language Paul appealed to them, while the local aristocracy spoke Latin and were for the most part poorly acquainted with Greek.

In Antioch it was that Paul turned entirely away from the Jews to the Gentiles; the step taken at Paphos was here carried to its proper completion. It was at Antioch, too, that the intermediate step was taken. On the first Sabbath after his arrival Paul preached to the mixed audience, and addressed them all as "Brethren" without distinction of race—the first occasion in the history of the Church when that was done frankly and without apology. Luke marks the importance of the step by giving a full résumé of the sermon. The step was not made from any preconceived design; incidentally, little by little, in the course of the sermon, Paul became conscious that it was being made as the Divine impulse drove him on. Addressing this new audience, he became sensitive as a true orator to something hitherto unknown to him in the character of his audience; and like an orator he adapted himself to it, "becoming all things to all men". He was aware of a certain sympathetic movement of spirit in the large Gentile part of his audience: this sympathy was the force that brought almost the whole city together a week later: it was already manifest on the first Sabbath:

it sprang from a certain affinity of character between the nature of the Anatolian people on the plateau and the Jews; Paul felt it first in Antioch and afterward in other Galatian cities. It was this same quality that a few years later inclined the Galatian Churches to adopt the whole Law and ritual of Judaism, and drew upon them the strong condemnation expressed in the letter to the Galatians.

This spirit in the pre-Roman population, the mass of the city, became the occasion of Paul's marked forward movement on the first Sabbath in Antioch. On the other hand, the Roman aristocracy of the Colony, sons of Western immigrants, had none of that affinity in spirit with the East, but retained their Western character.

The Jews, who were now thrown into hostility against Paul, took advantage of the division of feeling. The Romans held the reins of government, as the privileged class. To them the Jews went for aid, reaching them through the ladies of their order. Luke does not tell what formal charge was brought against Paul; but we can hardly doubt that he and Barnabas were accused of disturbing the harmony of the State, a vague yet a dangerous pretext, which brought about their expulsion.

Iconium, still called Konia, to which Paul and

Barnabas fled from Antioch, was not a Roman Colony but a Hellenized city, that is, a city in which Greek constitutional methods of government by elected magistrates had been established, and Greek civilization and education flourished. The people prided themselves that Iconium was the most ancient of cities, existing before, and rebuilt immediately after, the flood. The King of Iconium at the flood was Nannakos; and in Greece it became a proverbial expression for immemorial antiquity to say "older than Nannakos," as we say "before the flood" or "antediluvian".

In this belief that Iconium was the most ancient of cities, there is an interesting analogy with Damascus, where the same belief has always been held. The situation of the two cities is very similar. Each lies on a lofty level plain, Damascus 2300, Iconium 3370 feet above the sea. Each lies at the western edge of the plain, which stretches far away to the east, but is bounded by mountains a few miles to the west of the city. Each is well supplied with water that flows down from the mountains on the west; but the small streams that come to Iconium and are exhausted in the city cannot compare in size with the rivers that rush through Damascus to lose themselves in the thirsty plain on the east. Each city, however, profits by the abundant water; the fertile soil becomes a great garden; both are green with trees which are conspicuous in the distant view, and gladden the eyes of the traveller approaching across the dry plains. Yet there is no monotony in the view from either city across the vast plains, for character and variety are imparted by mountain peaks which rise sharply here and there like islands in an ocean.

Iconium and Damascus were also alike in being both cities rather of peace and commerce than of war. Neither could be made a strong city in ancient methods of warfare except by walls of vast size like those of Babylon; neither was guarded by difficult and steep approaches. Their importance lay in their productiveness and the wealth which they derived from agriculture and trade. Both must attract inhabitants from the beginning of organized human society, and their proud claim to vast antiquity was based on truth and fact. Damascus has bulked far more largely in the eyes of the world than Iconium, because it lay closer to the great peoples of ancient history, Jews, Assyrians, Babylonians, Egyptians, Arabs.

The problem of associating in one city the alien and often hostile minds and manners of Asiatics and Europeans was attempted in different ways at Iconium, at Antioch, and at Tarsus; but in all those great cities of Asia Minor the same problem was engaging attention, and varied constitutions and laws were framed to make possible a peaceful amalgamation of the diverse elements. In Iconium the Hellenic element consisted mainly of the educated and Hellenized part of the native population, with some immigrant Greeks. But it reckoned itself a Hellenic city, and its inhabitants are correctly called Hellenes by Luke, whereas he never uses that term about Antioch or Lystra, which were Roman Colonies.[1] Even in such a small detail as that he is strictly accurate.

Shortly before Paul visited Iconium the Emperor Claudius had observed and rewarded the loyalty of Iconium by granting to it the title Claudian; and it long was known as the city Claudiconium. This, however, did not make it a Roman Colony. It continued to be a Hellenic city throughout the

[1] While in Lystra there were a few Hellenes, the mass of the population were Lycaonians. In Pisidian Antioch the mass of the people were Phrygians, and in Philippi Macedonians; but a larger proportion of these had received a Greek education than in Lystra. In all such Colonies the non-Roman inhabitants were summed up in Latin as *plebs*, the plebeians or the multitude, and Luke employs the correct Greek term which was used regularly as a translation of *plebs*. Only in Corinth does he call the mass of the people Hellenes, though it was a Roman Colony; but in Corinth the whole mass of the population were Hellenes by blood and race, and in geographical fact.

time when Paul was visiting it (as is implied in Acts and as is proved by coins and inscriptions). Hadrian honoured it with the rank and privileges of a Colony about eighty years later.

Corresponding to the difference between Antioch, where an aristocracy of Roman colonists was the ruling influence, and Hellenic Iconium, where power lay with the whole body of citizens, were Paul's experiences in the two cities. From Antioch he had been expelled by Jewish foes who influenced the ladies of the aristocracy. In Iconium those enemies had to accomplish the same object by working on the feelings of the general body of citizens, which is a slower process; and while it was going on Paul "tarried there a long time speaking boldly". Gradually "the population of the city was divided, and part held with the Jews and part with the Apostles". The process is characteristic of popular government, such as Hellenic cities loved. Paul was thus able to stay a long time in Iconium; and it is not strange that the city appears in subsequent history as a very important Christian centre, sending its influence far through central Asia Minor.

Iconium was the last city of Phrygia; and the two Apostles after leaving it crossed the frontier and came into the region of Lycaonia with its two cities, Lystra and Derbe. There was another part of Lycaonia, which was not at that time within the Roman Empire, and therefore lay outside the limits which Paul set to his work. Lystra was, like Antioch, a Roman Colony, with a body of Roman settlers among a large population of rude Lycaonian rustics. It lay in an open valley among the hills, close to the junction of two streams which flow from the western mountains into the plain twenty miles south of Iconium. It never exercised much influence on the development of the country, but remained a small rural town to the end, always attracting some population and deriving moderate wealth from its fertile valley, but by its secluded position unsuited ever to become great. The character of this rude, uneducated country town appears in all Paul's adventures there. Though Greek was certainly the language in which he preached, yet Lycaonian, not Greek (which only educated people knew), was the language most familiar to his worshippers: Paul's appeal to them was in the simple style which suited a rustic people ; the populace was easily turned from the extreme of adoration to the extreme of hatred. There were some Hellenes in Lystra, among them Timothy, as we learn later, and Paul reached this educated class ; but on the whole he had not great success. Both the rude Lycaonian mob and the Roman aristocracy remained outside of his influence. It was the vigorous, progressive people of the middle class, fairly educated, but yet neither cultured dilettanti nor self-satisfied philosophers, among whom Paul found most hearers and converts, though there were in every city a few from the higher classes and a considerable number of the humblest attracted by his teaching.

Derbe, where Paul made many disciples, was a city of the open plain, on a great road. It derived some importance at this time from its position as a frontier city of the Empire, where customs had to be levied on imports, and business was active. But like Lystra it never became important in the history of the Church, and almost disappeared from notice during the fifth century and later. It is to us little more than a name.

The great service to Pauline study of fixing exactly the site of Lystra, and approximately that of Derbe, was rendered by an American scholar and traveller, Professor Sterrett of Cornell.

Ephesus, the commercial capital of the great and wealthy province of Asia, was not in Paul's time the official capital. Hence he never came in contact with the Governor of the province, as he did at Corinth with the Governor of Achaia and in Paphos with the Governor of Cyprus. It is quite clear that when the riot, which was caused by Demetrius and allayed by the secretary to the city, took place, there was no provincial Governor resident in Ephesus

The city, whose deserted site is now five miles from the sea, was in the first century a seaport, the most important in the whole of Asia. To the Romans, Asia was the name of the province which included the western part of Asia Minor: it was bounded on the east by the province of Galatia, and on the north by the Dardanelles and by the province of Bithynia; and it ranked as the most important in the Roman Empire, so far as education and wealth were concerned. Ephesus was the great harbour, at the old mouth of the Cayster, from which the products of both the province and many remoter parts of the continent of Asia were carried to Rome. It was the sea-end of great routes which stretched far away across Asia Minor and the Continent. It was the gate through which Asia looked out toward Europe. Hence already on his second journey Paul was evidently bent on entering the province Asia and going to Ephesus; but he was forbidden by Divine command to preach in the province Asia at that time, and was finally, after long wandering, conducted to Europe.

Owing to this change of plan on the second journey the advance of the new Faith beyond Galatia did not proceed evenly. Paul found himself following the line of the land-road from the

East to Rome, by way of Troas and Macedonia. Philippi and Amphipolis and Thessalonica lay on this land-road; and, for a time, it seemed as if Paul's work were to be carried on along its course; but again he was diverted from it, and at last he planted his feet firmly on the great central highway from the East by way of Ephesus and Corinth to Rome.

Corinth seems to have exercised a marked influence on Paul. There he came to realize that the Roman Imperial administration was the protector of the weak against the strong, and the maintainer of order and peace in the cities and the provinces. In the Hellenic cities the Jews or the mob could generally manage to sway the magistrates against a stranger like himself. Even in the Roman Colonies, Lystra, Pisidian Antioch, Philippi, the magistrates were too near the native character. But, when he reached the presence of the higher Roman officials, such as Sergius Paulus and Gallio, he experienced fair, sometimes even sympathetic treatment founded on wide general principles of policy and independent of narrow local interests and considerations. The scheme for the conquest of the Roman Empire now grew clearer in his mind . it had been present long ago to him, but now he saw the best means to that end, and he carried it out through all his future career.

Apart from this there is no proof that the special character or surroundings of Corinth exercised on Paul any serious influence. Especially, the theory that he was affected by its proximity to the seat of the Isthmian Games or of the Eleusinian Mysteries seems wholly groundless. There were Games and Mysteries in all parts of the Hellenic world; and Paul had long ago learned what their character was. The education and the superficial, rather conceited and opinionative philosophy, which was common in Corinth and Athens, exercised a repellent effect upon him. He recognized that the self-satisfied philosopher was the slowest to believe and the hardest to convince. But the position of Corinth as the key of communication along the central artery of the Empire, and as a point where many men from all quarters of the world met in passing, impressed on him the importance of constant intercourse and in the formation and maintenance of a world-wide Church.

On his third journey, after going through the Churches of Galatia, Paul went straight to Ephesus, visiting no other city by the way. He had learned ere this that the best way of reaching the people was not to go over the smaller cities one by one, but to proceed direct to the capital of each province. In the capital he had the opportunity of addressing, not merely the inhabitants of the city itself, but

LII. THE INFLUENCE OF LOCAL CIRCUMSTANCES

also numbers of people who for one reason or another came to the principal city, some for business, some for religion, some for law, some for education or curiosity. Especially the religion of the great goddess of Ephesus, Artemis or Diana, exercised a strong influence over the whole province Asia. Many people came on pilgrimage to worship. More came to see the magnificent ceremonies and splendid games, by which the magistrates and wealthy citizens honoured the festivals of Diana and made the city brilliant. Such magnificent ceremonies cost large sums of money; but the expenditure was productive, because hosts of visitors were attracted to the shows, and spent money freely in Ephesus. Here Paul established himself for a long residence, and exercised a strong influence on the people. Some of the chief men of the province, wealthy persons who were appointed priests in the worship paid by the province to the Roman Emperors as the embodiments of Divine power on earth, were his friends. The persons who practised magic, and who were also dabblers in science and investigators of the secrets of nature and practisers, of spiritualistic arts, found that their influence was much diminished.

The votaries of the goddess, who used to buy offerings to present to the goddess, now went to listen to Paul; and all the trades which ministered to the wants of devotees were seriously affected. The theatre, in which the rioters gathered to shout their adoration of the goddess and their hatred of Paul, is still a stately ruin of vast size; and a broad street leads down from its northern extremity to the ancient harbour (now a swamp covered with reeds).

Though Paul founded many other Churches in the province Asia, this was done through his helpers, such as Timothy, Titus, and others. He himself says that he had never seen the faces of the Colossians or the Laodiceans; but he wrote to them, and he sent envoys to speak in his name. Miletus, on the south shore of the gulf into which the Mæander used to fall, though its former shore-line is now many miles distant from the sea, because the river has filled completely up the gulf, Paul did visit more than once. His ship stayed there in A.D. 57, and the Ephesian elders came to hear his farewell message; and again years later, after he had returned from the great trial in Rome, we know that he was in Miletus and left his faithful friend Trophimus there sick.

Troas played the greatest part in Paul's life of all the cities in Asia except Ephesus. It was a Roman Colony, and a harbour of importance for communication with the coasts of Macedonia. It was also the sea-end of one or more roads from the

LII. THE INFLUENCE OF LOCAL CIRCUMSTANCES

northern parts of Asia Minor. Thus Paul came down to Troas on his second journey. There he found Luke. There he had the dream which beckoned him on into Europe. From Troas he sailed for Philippi. Again at a later date, when forced to leave Ephesus, he came to Troas intending to sail for Macedonia; but finding there an open door he stayed for some time in mission work. Again on his way to Jerusalem, he sailed from Macedonia to Troas. Many years later, he again visited this important harbour in his progress round the Ægean Churches; and there he left the cloak, whose want he felt in the winter following.

In this review of the geographical surroundings amid which Paul's life was spent, we see how the human spirit gradually emancipates itself from the influence of external circumstances and attains to dominion over them. It is evident that the conditions of life in Tarsus and Jerusalem had great effect in forming Paul's views and opinions. As his character grew stronger and his outlook on the world gained breadth he gradually learned to use for his purposes geographical and other external conditions. All the resources of civilization, all the opportunities of life, were employed by him with ever-increasing skill and ever-widening experience to further his aims. The pressure of external conditions drove him to Pisidian Antioch, yet in that region he made the conditions subservient to his plans. During the latter part of his career it is evident that in such cities as Ephesus and Troas it was no longer the local circumstances which moulded him, but he who employed the local circumstances for the advantage of his work. He used the opportunities of nature, the "open door," with the genius of a great administrator.

www.ingramcontent.com/pod-product-compliance
Lightning Source LLC
Chambersburg PA
CBHW071225230426
43668CB00011B/1312